WHAT

BIBLE SEX DEVOTIONAL

- Rene and Gloria, (We) have been greatly encouraged by your blog posts, can't wait to get a copy of your book. Thank you for thoughtfully addressing the topic of sex in these ways! - Sam R
- This is really cool! I'm getting married in 24 days and my fiance and I just talked about this in our premarital counseling. This is a relatively new view of sex for me; I think this is an awesome understanding. - Nathan M
- You guys are amazing and this is a wonderful subject you are teaching on. It's so taboo, so it's never taught, but it should be! Christians shouldn't be uneducated on sex because sex is typically viewed as a bad, immoral thing. Biblical sex should be taught MORE because I believe it is one huge key to a long successful marriage in world where the divorce rate is 50/50. Thank you so much for what you both are doing!! - Jacqueline E
- Hi there, My husband and I are going through rough patch in our marriage and this is exactly what we needed to read. We are well on our way to mending things, but after

10 years of being together, 4 years married, we are just now truly learning each other sexually. Your blog is exactly what we needed for this time in our marriage. So thank you so much for putting this out there and taking a risk to teach on such a taboo subject. How can I get a copy of your book/books? After reading the blog, my husband and I are craving more in depth teaching on this so we can have a marriage the way God truly intended. - J.E.

- I am loving the truth you are sharing - some is new to me although maybe just a different way of understanding the truth - and some is a great reminder! THANK YOU! - Yancey C.
- I love how simple God's way is compared to the complicated human way. - Chris B.
- Thank you! Great read on how and why marriages fail due to sexual sin. You have written a needed book in this world of unfulfilled married couples. Thank you! - Elaine M., author
- Good stuff -- very insightful! - Jim W., pastor
- Rene and Gloria are good friends who have some good insights into marriage. I appreciate their candor and openness and would recommend that you sign up for their devotional. - Davis Mc, pastor
- Love your site!!! So well written. Thank you! - Anon
- Read through every single post on your blog.

Truly amazing. I'm also encouraging those to join your FB group. - Anon
- My husband and I are currently reading Sheet Music by Dr. Kevin Leman along with all the post/blogs you guys write and we are loving it! We are seeing sex in such a different light; it is drastically changing our relationship and sex life, for the better! - J.E.
- You have an important mission. As a Christian sex and relationship coach it warms my heart to see ministers such as yourselves reaching out to help those in need. Be blessed. - Micki A.
- I enjoyed your blog post, I read multiple blogs...good work... :) love they are based off scripture!! :) - Alisha, Twitter follower
- This sweet couple go to our church in SLC and are in the process of publishing a book. Check them out and follow them to support their efforts in redeeming a topic that culture has destroyed. - Matthew M.
- Love love love what you guys are doing and I look forward to all of your posts! Keep on keeping on because you all are making a difference! - FB

BOOKS AND RESOURCES BY RENÉ &
GLORIA VALLIÈRES

RADICAL SEX: GOD'S FOUNDATION FOR A HEALTHY MARRIAGE

40 DAY BIBLE SEX DEVOTIONAL FOR CHRISTIAN COUPLES

14 DAY BIBLE SEX DEVOTIONAL FOR CHRISTIAN COUPLES (EBOOK ONLY)

5 FALSE ASSUMPTIONS CHRISTIAN COUPLES MAKE ABOUT MARRIED SEX (*FREE* EREPORT)

HOW TO LEAD YOUR SMALL GROUP INTO THE PRESENCE OF GOD

ALL BOOKS AND RESOURCES AVAILABLE THROUGH WWW.THEBIBLESEXDEVOTIONAL.COM

40 DAY BIBLE SEX DEVOTIONAL

FOR CHRISTIAN COUPLES

RENE & GLORIA VALLIERES

40 Day Bible Sex Devotional for Christian Couples

www.thebiblesexdevotional.com

Copyright © 2018 by Rene & Gloria Vallieres

All rights reserved.

Independently Published

Unless otherwise noted, Scripture quotations are from the Holy Bible, English Standard Version®, © 2001 by Crossway Bibles, a publishing ministry of Good News Publishers.

Italicized words in Scripture quotes are the emphasis of the authors.

Front Cover Illustration by Christine Vallieres

Unauthorized use and/or duplication of this material without express and written permission from the authors and/or owner is strictly prohibited. Excerpts and links may be used, provided that full and clear credit is given to Rene and Gloria Vallieres with appropriate and specific direction to the original content including title.

 Created with Vellum

For our grandchildren and their future spouses

CONTENTS

Preface   xi
Introduction   xiii

Day 1 - No Sex, No Marriage	1
Day 2 - "I now Pronounce You Best Friends Forever!"	3
Day 3 - "Sex is Dirty"	5
Day 4 - They're Only Good for One Thing	7
Day 5 - 5 False Assumptions about Married Sex	9
Day 6 - The Only Reason to Get Married	12
Day 7 - Sex & Sanctification	15
Day 8 - SOS & SEX	18
Day 9 - An Ice Cream Sundae Marriage	22
Day 10 - The Sex Bus	25
Day 11 - "I Do!" Means "I Will!"	28
Day 12 - An Inconvenient Truth	31
Day 13 - Casual Sex	34
Day 14 - Intoxication	37
Day 15 - 7 Lessons from Numbers 25	40
Day 16 - The Royal Wedding	43
Day 17 - The Death of Sex	46
Day 18 - Mostly Dead Sex Life	49
Day 19 - 3 Enemies of Sex	52
Day 20 - Petri Dish for Porn	56
Day 21 - The Last Taboo	60
Day 22 - Loving the Unlovable Lover	63
Day 23 - There's More to Life than Sex!	66
Day 24 - Have Sex to Forget about Sex	69
Day 25 - Pay Attention	72
Day 26 - Get Uncomfortable	75
Day 27 - Satan's Wish List	78

Day 28 - Life is Short	82
Day 29 - Marriage: God's Boot Camp	85
Day 30 - How to Be Sex-Positive	88
Day 31 - Attitude is Everything	91
Day 32 - Men and Women are Different	94
Day 33 - Diluted Senses	98
Day 34 - Lasting Love Must be Taught	102
Day 35 - How to Talk about You Know What	106
Day 36 - The Marital Rights of the Wife	110
Day 37 - The First Command of God to His Children	113
Day 38 - Joyfully Stuck!	116
Day 39 - Not in the Mood	120
Day 40 - God Sees Us as One	123
Afterword	127
Notes	129
About the Authors	130

PREFACE

The devotionals in this volume were originally published on our blog. After about 30 posts or so, we realized new visitors were having trouble picking up posts from the beginning since most of the posts were archived. So we took them off the web site and put them in this volume for convenience and continuity. There are some editorial changes but they are largely what appeared on our web site. We're not sure if we will continue to blog or not but there will be no more devotionals like these.

 We feel, because of the personal nature of the studies, that they would be more helpful to Christian couples in one volume either in print, or eBook, format so they could be read together. It seems to us that it's a better alternative than searching through archives on a web site trying to get the posts in the proper order. The devotionals can be taken individually but they were intended to build on each other from one to forty.

PREFACE

We submit these meditations for your encouragement and pray these humble studies will help you, as a couple, grow in the grace and knowledge of our Lord and Savior Jesus Christ. May they, in some small way, contribute to your marriage going from good to great. To God be the glory!

- Rene and Gloria Vallieres, Christmas 2018

INTRODUCTION

Marriage is in trouble. Marriage rates are down, divorce rates continue to be high. Many Christian husbands are turning to pornography while most wives are dissatisfied with their sex lives. Communication breakdowns, stresses of modern life, and easy access to pornography continue to sabotage Christian marriages.

What is the solution?

We believe God's solution is *Radical Sex*. *Radical Sex* is God's way for his married children that cuts through secular philosophies and false piety. God is a practical God who, through his Word, provides clear instruction about every area of our lives including sex.

Radical by David Platt calls Christians to live like Jesus and drop all the pretenses of "The American Dream". It has over 1,500 positive reviews on Amazon! Francis Chan, a popular author, also calls Christians to live a radical lifestyle for Jesus. Many Christian authors

INTRODUCTION

call us to love our neighbors, make disciples, and live intentionally, or missional, for Jesus.

We believe we should live radically with our spouse first. Love your spouse radically, God's way. What is more radical than to make love to your spouse frequently and reciprocally?

Tim and Kathy Keller say sex in a Christian marriage should be "frequent and reciprocal."[1] Fair enough, but what does that mean? It begs the question, *How frequent, and how reciprocal?* We attempt to answer this important question.

Actually, we'll let you in on a secret: What we call *Radical Sex* is God's *Normal Sex*. It's radical to us because we have gotten so far from God's intention for sex in marriage. Frequent and reciprocal sex sounds extreme but it wasn't always this way. The Bible makes it clear that frequent, we mean *very* frequent, reciprocal sex is God's way to a healthy marriage and our personal holiness. We cover all this in detail in our book, **Radical Sex: God's Foundation for a Healthy Marriage**.

It's easy to get excited about living radically for Jesus but sometimes hard to love the one you're with day in and day out. Let's start to live for Jesus with our spouse and then we can go out and save the world. If we can't love our spouses radically how can we love others radically?

Why I Hate Religion, But Love Jesus has over 32 million views on YouTube. Whether you agree with the sentiment or not, it resonates with a lot of people. People are sick of false religious piety and long for something genuine and authentic.

Nearly every Christian book on marriage includes an

INTRODUCTION

obligatory chapter on sex that says, "God created sex!" and "God loves sex!" and "You should do it more!" But it's a lot easier said than done. Our books help you think biblically about sex and rely on the Holy Spirit to help you do married sex God's way. Join the movement to bring married sex into the light of the gospel.

This volume captures the spirit of our book *Radical Sex* in an easy to read format with 40 short devotionals. We encourage you to get the book also which goes into biblical married sex with much more depth. The book covers everything you ever wanted to know about what God thinks of sex but were afraid to ask.

We sadly recognize that many women—and some men as well—are in abusive relationships. According to one study, as many as one in four Christian marriages are unhealthy to the point of abuse. If you are in an abusive relationship, we plead with you to talk to your pastor, law enforcement officials, or a qualified counselor. Get help and be safe.

This devotional, and our book, is not for the 25% in difficult and sometimes dangerous relationships, but for the 75% of Christian marriages which are essentially healthy, but want more out of their marriages. Sex God's way is *not* the answer to *every* marital problem; although, in our opinion, it helps remove 90% of the daily mutual annoyances and irritations. If you have major issues in your marriage, seek counseling first. But if you are part of the 75% of Christian marriages that want to go from good to great then follow God's marriage instructions.

Follow us at *TheBibleSexDevotional.com*

DAY 1 - NO SEX, NO MARRIAGE

Then Jacob said to Laban, "Give me my wife. My time is completed, and I want to make love to her." So Laban brought together all the people of the place and gave a feast. But when evening came, he took his daughter Leah and brought her to Jacob, and Jacob made love to her. When morning came, there was Leah! So Jacob said to Laban, "What is this you have done to me? I served you for Rachel, didn't I? Why have you deceived me?" Laban replied, "It is not our custom here to give the younger daughter in marriage before the older one." (Genesis 29:21-23,25,26 NIV)

Jacob made love to Leah and, Voila!, they were married. He didn't try to persuade Laban to take Leah back. Jacob understood sex sealed the deal.

Everyone knows, and has since the beginning of time, that the consummation makes a marriage, not the engagement, vows, rings, or ceremonies. Sex does and only sex. In fact, you can get married, and live together for years, but if you never had sex no one considers you really married - church, society, or God.

In times past, Kings and Queens were subjected to a public consummation event at the end of the marriage ceremony to assure it was a "real" marriage. The political powers wanted to make sure the marriage alliance was not a sham.

Paul calls the physical union of a man and a woman a "profound mystery" because it's God's metaphor for the union of Christ and his followers. (See Ephesians 5:31,32) This speaks primarily to the covenant element of both relationships but more on this later.

Bible Thought: Sex is much more than a physical union.

Prayer: Father, help me to understand your purpose for sex in my marriage. In Jesus' name. Amen.

DAY 2 - "I NOW PRONOUNCE YOU BEST FRIENDS FOREVER!"

When Rachel saw that she bore Jacob no children, she envied her sister. She said to Jacob, "Give me children, or I shall die!" Jacob's anger was kindled against Rachel, and he said, "Am I in the place of God, who has withheld from you the fruit of the womb?" (Genesis 30:1,2 ESV)

The officiant of your wedding probably didn't declare at the end of the ceremony, "I now pronounce you BFF's!" but many anniversary posts suggest otherwise.

Anyone who has been married a while understands that your spouse can be your best friend one moment and your worst enemy the next. Jacob was intoxicated with Rachel and waited 7 years (actually 14) to "make love" to her and "they seemed like only a few days to him because of his love for her." (Genesis 29:20b ESV)

In the very next chapter, they seem to loathe one another. "Jacob's anger was kindled against Rachel". Rachel wasn't much better. What happened? They had the dreaded "sex conversation". "Give me children, or I shall die!" Granted, it wasn't the usual modern sex discussion about frequency or reciprocity. It was more, "It's your fault I'm not pregnant!" Jacob took exception.

As we saw in the Day 1 entry, marriage is an exclusive, covenant relationship unlike any other. Friendship is wonderful, and hopefully, you and your spouse exhibit the traits of best friends - love, respect, loyalty.

Please don't be offended with our BFF fun. We understand why you post, "I married my best friend!" But let's not forget our spouse is our covenant partner first and foremost. The covenant was sealed with sex in the beginning and is renewed with each subsequent encounter.

When we don't have frequent sex with our spouse, our covenant relationship fades into a distant, foggy memory. Each sexual encounter reminds us of our exclusive relationship. Sadly, we tend to forget quickly!

BIBLE THOUGHT: Frequent sex with our spouse reminds us of our exclusive, covenant relationship.

PRAYER: Father, you created marriage and sex. Help me to dig into the Word and discover what you say about marriage and sex. In Jesus' name. Amen.

DAY 3 - "SEX IS DIRTY"

But sexual immorality and all impurity or covetousness must not even be named among you, as is proper among saints. (Ephesians 5:3 ESV)

We know sex is a difficult subject for a lot of us. After all there are many verses like the one above. We are conditioned to suppress, deny, ignore wayward sexual thoughts. If that doesn't work then keep as distracted as possible. It's no wonder Christians avoid thinking about sex let alone talking about sex. This conditioning of not thinking about sex and not talking about sex kills intimacy in many marriages.

A lot of Christians think "sex" is a dirty word. Some consequently think sex is dirty. Pornography sells dirty sex and millions are buying it perverting God's purpose for sex. God makes sex pure in marriage and uses it for our good and his glory.

We may have struggled with the place of sex in our lives, marriages, and minds. Everywhere we turn, we're reminded of the sexual failure of our past.

Our sexual history, for most of us, is a strange journey. As we look back we realize that before marriage, the enemy tempted us with the thrill of sex and then after marriage he reverses his tactics to convince us sex is boring and watching Netflix is more exciting. God's way is the opposite where the real thrill of marriage is sex between a committed, covenant couple in Christ.

Let's think about sex the way God thinks about sex. Let's talk about sex the way God talks about sex. And let's start in our own homes with our spouses. Most sex conversations are difficult but if we're not talking about sex then we're probably not doing it.

BIBLE THOUGHT: God makes sex pure in marriage.

PRAYER: Father, show me what you think about sex. Help me to renew my mind about sex from your Word. In Jesus' name. Amen.

DAY 4 - THEY'RE ONLY GOOD FOR ONE THING

Now Laban had two daughters; the name of the older was Leah, and the name of the younger was Rachel. Leah had weak eyes, but Rachel had a lovely figure and was beautiful. (Genesis 29:16-17 NIV)

Jacob is completely smitten with Rachel's beauty and especially her "lovely figure". He is so smitten that he offered to work for seven years for Rachel. When the seven years are up he tells Laban, "Give me my wife. My time is completed, and I want to make love to her." (v 21)

God has given most men a strong sex drive, a *very* strong sex drive. A strong sex drive is not lust, it is a gift from God and like all divine gifts it can misused. Men behaving badly is in the news but it's nothing new. God gave Jacob a strong sexual desire for Rachel but he didn't use it until they were married.

Lust selfishly desires something or someone and takes it greedily at all cost as soon as possible. Love considers the interest of the other greater than their own and gives generously. (See Philippians 2:4)

For example, a husband can objectify his wife when he sees her as "only good for one thing". However, a wife can objectify her husband with the same thought "he's only good for one thing". Anytime we detach our spouse from the "one flesh" reality of marriage, and objectify them, we perpetuate the wrong idea that marriage is made up of two autonomous people, living separate lives, for the primary purpose of my convenience, and self satisfaction.

Does a healthy husband want to have sex with his wife? Does it necessarily follow that he only sees her as a sexual object? Does a wife want her husband to care for the kids and help pay the rent? Does it necessarily follow that she only sees him as a babysitter and a bank?

BIBLE THOUGHT: Love gives, lust takes.

PRAYER: Father, show me the difference between love and lust. Keep me from lust and help me to truly love my spouse. In Jesus' name. Amen.

DAY 5 - 5 FALSE ASSUMPTIONS ABOUT MARRIED SEX

Wisdom Speaking
I love those who love me,
and those who seek me diligently find me.
(Proverbs 8:17 ESV)

We would all agree that we need God's wisdom to navigate marriage successfully. We started the blog, and wrote the book ***Radical Sex: God's Foundation for a Healthy Marriage***, because we didn't always get it right. By God's grace, we learned a few things over the years and want to share them with those who seek to do marriage God's way.

The good news is that God will give us his wisdom if we want it. Mark Driscoll says, "The 'want to' has to come before the 'how to'." Do you want to do it God's way?

Let's start by looking at five wrong assumptions many of us make.

1. **We say** we got married because we were in love, best friends, and wanted to build a life together (and so many other reasons). **God says** sex is the only reason you need to get married.
2. **We say** sex is for procreation first and then pleasure. **God says** sex is for our sanctification first.
3. **We say** sex is primarily for men and secondarily for women. **God says** sex is for both husband and wife equally.
4. **We say** sex is one of many elements that make up a happy marriage. **God says** sex is the first priority of a happy marriage.
5. **We say** we overcome sexual temptation through spiritual warfare: prayer, fasting, self control, anti-porn software, accountability partners, expensive DVD's, and will power. **God says** the best way to overcome sexual temptation is frequent and reciprocal married sex.

These are just a few of the wrong assumptions we make about married sex. We will look at each in detail from the Bible in the next few devotionals.

Are we married sex experts? No, not at all! But God is! And, fortunately, he tells us how to do it in his Word; that is, if we "want to".

. . .

BIBLE THOUGHT: God knows us better than we know ourselves.

PRAYER: Father, I assume many things that are contrary to your truth. Help we to put down my assumptions about sex and take up your truth. In Jesus' name. Amen.

DAY 6 - THE ONLY REASON TO GET MARRIED

> *Now concerning the matters about which you wrote: "It is good for a man not to have sexual relations with a woman." But because of the temptation to sexual immorality, each man should have his own wife and each woman her own husband.* (1 Corinthians 7:1,2 ESV)

False Assumption #1: **We say** we got married because we were in love, best friends, and wanted to build a life together (and so many other reasons). **God says** sex is the only reason you need to get married.

The quote in verse 1 is from the hyper-spiritual, gnostic, faction at Corinth that taught sexual self-control was the holier way. After all, Christianity is a spiritual religion that renounces all things of the flesh. Right?

Paul exposes their wrong thinking by pointing out our extreme sexual weakness and, then, stating clearly that the antidote to sexual temptation is *not* abstinence, but the very opposite. Paul, in effect, says "Stop spiritualizing everything! The physical is not evil."

Paul then says that if you're struggling with sexual temptation then get married. Marriage is God's only solution to sexual temptation and the primary reason to get married. There are many reasons why people get married but if one spouse gets married to overcome sexual temptation and other spouse gets married for any other reason then that's a problem.

"But because of the temptation to sexual immorality, each man should have his own wife and each woman her own husband." This is a message to men and women, equally.

The opposite is also true; that is, if you don't suffer from sexual temptation then don't get married. Paul goes on to say that a single person can serve the Lord wholeheartedly but a married person must be "anxious" about serving their spouse. (See 1 Corinthians 7:32-35 ESV)

Sex is the only reason to get married, or more accurately, the only reason you ***need*** to get married as a Christian. You can do everything as an unmarried couple, that you can do as a married couple, except have sex according to the Bible.

Think about it. You can be best friends, enjoy shared interests, go on dates, and laugh at each other's jokes. You can even be roommates and raise a family by adopting children. You can do it all without being married. Sex is the only reason to get married as Christians.

. . .

Bible Thought: God loves the physical; after all, he made the earth and all things in it. "God saw all that He had made, and behold, it was very good." (See Genesis 1:31a NASB)

Prayer: Father, you made all things including sex between a husband and wife and declared it as "very good". Help me to see sex as "very good" like you do. In Jesus' name. Amen.

DAY 7 - SEX & SANCTIFICATION

> *For this is the will of God, your sanctification: that you abstain from sexual immorality; that each one of you know how to control his own body in holiness and honor ...* (1 Thessalonians 4:3-4 ESV)

False Assumption #2: **We say** sex is for procreation first and then pleasure. **God says** sex is for our sanctification first.

God's will is that we overcome sexual temptation by acquiring a wife or by learning to live with our wife. What happens when we acquire a wife or learn to live with our wife? God says we can then move forward in a life pleasing to him, or our "sanctification".

Sanctification simply means to be "set apart for God's purpose". It also has the idea of "growing in grace" or maturing in Christ. Paul says the first step in "walking in the Spirit", another way of describing sanctification, is to deal with the 800 pound animal in the room - sexual temptation.

> *That each one of you know how to control his own body in holiness and honor.*

Paul lays out the only two options for overcoming sexual temptation. He uses a common idiom that covers both single and married persons, literally "possess your own vessel". Paul is saying that if you are single then "learn to acquire a wife" (alternate reading); and if you are married then, "learn to live with your own wife," (alternate reading; see 1 Thessalonians 4:4 notes)

Paul is addressing men but the principles are the same for women - marriage and only marriage is God's solution to overcoming sexual temptation. We saw in our last entry that Paul addresses both men and women. In our passage today, Paul includes the idea that overcoming sexual temptation is the first, and perhaps the hardest, of all temptations.

Why is Paul addressing men primarily? Men are more inclined to make a mess of things as we've seen in the news lately although women are not immune.

This answer raises additional questions.

What does it mean to "acquire a wife"? This is the easy one: If you're single and struggling with sexual temptation then get married. We understand that it's easier said than done. So pray and get started!

What does Paul mean by "learn to live with your own

wife"? This is a little more complicated. We will look into this in a later entry.

But the clear indication is that husbands and wives do not automatically know how to live with one another. It has to be learned and that's exactly why we wrote our book, ***Radical Sex***.[1] We pray God will use it to help couples learn to live with each other in a life pleasing to God.

BIBLE THOUGHT: God's wants us to learn how to live with each other.

PRAYER: Father, sex is amazing but complicated. You made it simple but we complicate it. Help me to grow in your grace in my marriage. In Jesus' name. Amen.

DAY 8 - SOS & SEX

The Song of Songs, which is Solomon's.
The Bride Confesses Her Love
She
Let him kiss me with the kisses of
his mouth!
For your love is better than wine;
your anointing oils are fragrant;
your name is oil poured out;
therefore virgins love you.
Draw me after you; let us run.
The king has brought me into his
chambers. *(Song of Solomon 1:1-4 ESV)*

False Assumption #3: **We say** sex is primarily for men and secondarily for women. **God says** sex is for both husband and wife equally.

S.O.S is an international signal of distress. S.O.S, or Song of Solomon, is God's remedy for marital distress. This fascinating book of the Bible may not be easy to understand but it's Principles of Sexual Love are loud and clear. Married sex is for both men and women - equally. However, this book also makes it clear that men and women view sex differently.

The Word never even hints that sex is primarily for men and secondarily for women. Leah and Rachel fought over Jacob's sexual attentions. Sarah laughed after being told she would have "pleasure" in her old age, "After I am worn out, and my lord is old, shall I have pleasure?" (Genesis 18:12 ESV) The woman in the Song of Solomon is "intoxicated" with sexual desire for her husband (v2).

Today many, both men and women, see sex as primarily for the husband and a duty for the wife?

So what happened?

Here are a few wrong ideas about married sex that have undermined God's intended purpose.

- The culture demonizes men's natural sexual aggression and calls it "toxic". (It is toxic if misused but joyful if used with love in marriage.)
- The church agrees with the culture and promotes a "toxic" view of a strong sex drive often calling it "lust". (A strong sex drive is a wonderful gift from God.)
- The church promotes sexual restraint in marriage as a sign of greater holiness. (The

opposite is true: sexual restraint in marriage promotes sexual sin, not holiness.)
- Christian wives are encouraged to "help" their husbands control their unwieldy sex drive by suppressing all sensuality. (Again, the opposite is true: Wives are to encourage their husband's strong sex drive and fan it into flames to the delight of them both. (See SOS 4:9-10) She "captivates" his heart with her sexual love.)
- Men and women don't see sex as a primary reason for marriage. (Sex is the only reason a Christian couple *needs* to get married in the first place according to the Bible.)

As we are influenced by these non-biblical ideas, we will correspondingly think sex is primarily for men. The closer we get to God's model for sexual love in the Song of Solomon, we will see that sex is a fountain of joy for both men and women.

As we mentioned in the last entry, a biblical view of married sex has to be learned, it is not naturally acquired as we may think. The first step in learning about married sex is to *unlearn* our false cultural and religious assumptions. Look to God's Word for the truth that will set you free.

Bible Thought: God loves passion and encourages husbands and wives to fan it into flames.

. . .

Prayer: Father, help me to get closer to the sexual love model in the Song of Solomon. I turn to you, and your grace, to help me to understand you are for sex and not against sex in marriage. In Jesus' name. Amen.

DAY 9 - AN ICE CREAM SUNDAE MARRIAGE

Therefore a man shall leave his father and his mother and hold fast to his wife, and they shall become one flesh. (Genesis 2:24 ESV)

False Assumption #4: **We say** sex is one of many elements that make up a happy marriage. **God says** sex is the first priority of a happy marriage.

It's easy to get the impression from the culture and the church that marriage is like an ice cream sundae made up of lots of good things like friendship, shared interests, careers, and kids with sex as the cherry on top.

God says sex is not the cherry on top, it's the dish that holds the ice cream sundae.

We talk about communication, selflessness, perseverance, spiritual maturity, and other lofty elements as the essentials of a biblical marriage. God defines marriage in terms of a physical union.

God's definition of marriage is "one flesh". He could have described marriage as "one soul" or "one mind" as in "they shall become one mind" but he didn't. Some experts tell us the Hebrew word means more than a physical union.

However, Jesus says, "'Therefore a man shall leave his father and his mother and hold fast to his wife, and the two shall become *one flesh*'? So they are no longer two but *one flesh*." (Matthew 19 5,6a ESV emphasis added)

Jesus was having a discussion with the Pharisees about marriage and divorce. Jesus highlights the seriousness of divorce by revealing what God thinks about marriage. He seems to be saying, "How can you separate *one flesh*?"

He quotes Genesis 2:24 directly and then adds his own take, "So they are no longer two but *one flesh*" as if to remind the Pharisees of the essence of marriage. Whenever Jesus says the same thing twice in a row, he considers it important, very important. We should pay extra attention.

The Greek word used here, *sarx*, means "flesh, physical body, human nature". Strong defines this word as, "Flesh - the soft substance of the living body, which covers the bones and is permeated with blood of both man and beast". This doesn't sound like "one soul" or "one mind" to us!

Is marriage more than a physical union? Of course, the mystery of "one flesh" extends beyond sexual union to leaving and cleaving and building a separate family together. But "one flesh" is the picture of marriage God gives us and we ignore this divine emphasis to our own marital peril.

BIBLE THOUGHT: Sex is the cup that holds the ice cream sundae. Drop the cup and you have a mess to clean up.

PRAYER: Father, help me to make you my *first* priority with my spouse next. Help me to understand what makes up a biblical marriage for your glory. In Jesus' name. Amen.

DAY 10 - THE SEX BUS

The husband should give to his wife her conjugal rights, and likewise the wife to her husband. For the wife does not have authority over her own body, but the husband does. Likewise the husband does not have authority over his own body, but the wife does. Do not deprive one another, except perhaps by agreement for a limited time, that you may devote yourselves to prayer; but then come together again, so that Satan may not tempt you because of your lack of self-control. (1 Corinthians 7:3-5 ESV)

False Assumption #5: **We say** we overcome sexual temptation through spiritual warfare: prayer, fasting, self control, anti-porn software, accountability partners, expensive DVD's, and will power. **God says** the best way to overcome sexual temptation is frequent and reciprocal married sex.

WHO GETS to drive the sex bus?

We are encouraged to negotiate the frequency of sex by both Christian and secular marriage counselors. This is a self evident truth. What could be more obvious than a compromise on the frequency of sex in a loving marriage. Each marriage has its own rhythm after all, and we all know that negotiation and compromise are at the heart of a healthy marriage. This sounds reasonable, of course, until you realize intense sexual desire is neither reasonable nor negotiable.

What ends up happening, more often than not, is the one with the lower sex drive gets to set the frequency of sex in a marriage. God says clearly in today's passage that, in a biblical marriage, the one with the *higher sex drive* gets to drive the sex bus.

Husbands usually have the higher sex drive, but not always, and it varies in different seasons of marriage and from day to day especially as you get older. This is why Paul speaks to both husbands and wives, "Do not deprive one another."

So what happens if the lower sex drive spouse is driving the sex bus? Typically, the higher sex drive spouse tries to mitigate temptation with all kinds of spiritual self-help techniques. Entire ministries are built around the "other spouse" and their plight. Prayer, Bible study, anti-porn software, accountability partners, expensive DVD series are set in place to overcome sexual temptation for the spouse with the higher sex drive but relegated to the passenger seat.

We are all for prayer, Bible study, and accountability but not for overcoming sexual temptation in marriage.

Do these spiritual self-help methods work? They could be of some benefit in the short term, or if you're single, but God has a better way of overcoming sexual temptation for those of us who are married - frequent and reciprocal sex in a loving covenant relationship.

Pauls says, "Do not deprive one another."

Why does he say this?

Because he knows we tend to deprive one another.

BIBLE THOUGHT: The spouse with the higher sex drive gets to drive the sex bus in a biblical marriage.

PRAYER: Father, help me fight sexual temptation your way. Help me to help my spouse in their battle with sexual sin. In Jesus' name. Amen.

DAY 11 - "I DO!" MEANS "I WILL!"

The husband should give to his wife her conjugal rights, and likewise the wife to her husband. For the wife does not have authority over her own body, but the husband does. Likewise the husband does not have authority over his own body, but the wife does. (1 Corinthians 7:3,4 ESV)

Remember saying, "I do"?

Did any of us understand the sexual implications of that promise on our wedding day? Certainly not many, and not fully, we suspect. We didn't.

The moment you said "I do" you gave up a lot of your rights and took on a lot of responsibilities by your own free will. Your conjugal rights became your spouse's responsibility and your spouse's conjugal rights became your responsibility. Essentially, you became responsible for your spouse's sex life when you said "I do". Whoa, I didn't plan on that!

For example, the moment you are brought into the Kingdom by God, you are no longer your own but bought with a price by the shed blood of Jesus. (See 1 Corinthians 6:19,20 ESV) In a similar way, the moment you said "I do", you are no longer your own.

"For the wife does not have authority over her own body, but the husband does. Likewise the husband does not have authority over his own body, but the wife does." You are now part of a unique union called "one flesh" by God.

At the moment of your vow, and subsequent consummation, your body was united to our spouse's body in "one flesh". This is your new status.

Your status was "single" but now your status is "one flesh" from God's perspective on marriage.

Each spouse is now responsible, not only for their own body, but for their lover's body as well. On the other side, each spouse now freely surrenders their body to their spouse in fulfillment of their wedding vow, "I do!".

The responsibility now is to nourish and encourage each other, never to put down, deprive, or abuse.

Giving control of your body to someone else is not natural, it is supernatural! We can't do this on our own. We need Jesus and his gospel. Be patient, pray and trust God.

. . .

Bible Thought: The moment you said, "I do" you gave up many rights and took on many responsibilities.

Prayer: Father, help me to fulfill my responsibilities toward my spouse with kindness and love. In Jesus' name. Amen.

DAY 12 - AN INCONVENIENT TRUTH

> *The husband should give to his wife her conjugal rights, and likewise the wife to her husband. For the wife does not have authority over her own body, but the husband does. Likewise the husband does not have authority over his own body, but the wife does.* (1 Corinthians 7:3,4 ESV)

A refugee coming to America after escaping a war torn country observed that Americans' greatest fear is being inconvenienced. God's Word is more often than not going to be inconvenient. "Go and make disciples of all nations." Inconvenient, Lord!

Paul tells married people in these verses to prepare to be inconvenienced. He leaves no wiggle room to get out of sex. Your spouse has the right to sex whenever they want it and, oh, by the way you don't have authority over your body, your spouse does. Later in the passage he tells us the only time *not* to have sex is for a special time of prayer. Paul triple downs on frequent sex in marriage. He boxes us in with no way out. How inconvenient, Paul.

We love sex on cruises, in hotel rooms while on vacation, and sex when we want it. But sex whenever my spouse wants it, in everyday life, well, it's inconvenient and *unreasonable*.

What about negotiations? What if I'm not in the mood? Or exhausted? Or had a bad day? Paul says too bad, so sad. Sex is sometimes going to be inconvenient.

Wait a minute! Hold on! This sounds like sex on-demand.

"Sex on-demand" is like the sound of finger nails dragging across a chalk board to our postmodern ears. We are free, autonomous people after all. God says you *were* free and autonomous; that is, before you got married.

Paul's not talking about bullying, coercion, or abuse. It's estimated that 25% of married Christians are in abusive situations. If this is you then get help. Be safe. We're talking to the other 75% of Christian marriages who want their marriages to reflect God's purpose for marriage.

Biblical married sex is not natural, it is supernatural. We need God's help to do married sex his way. God wants to bring us out of our self-focused world of sin and into an other-focused world of love. Marriage apparently is one of the best way to learn how to really love.

Applying the truth of married sex will be inconvenient but full of blessings.

BIBLE THOUGHT: Our spouse's conjugal right is God's way of turning us from ourselves to another, our spouse, in married love.

PRAYER: Father, help me to respect and love my spouse in Christ. I acknowledge I need your help in this. In Jesus' name. Amen.

DAY 13 - CASUAL SEX

Do not deprive one another, except perhaps by agreement for a limited time, that you may devote yourselves to prayer; but then come together again, so that Satan may not tempt you because of your lack of self-control. (1 Corinthians 7:5 ESV emphasis added)

---

*E*verything seems to come before sex even Netflix, or should we say, especially Netflix. Today's headline is "Netflix is Killing Couple's Sex Lives: Study".[1] It goes on to describe the disturbing trend that couples are turning off the TV and going to bed with their iPads. Apparently, a decline in sex is corresponding with increased Netflix viewing in bed according to a university study. We even give it a name, "Netflix and Chill".

Sex has become casual for married couples. We take it as something we'll get around to eventually unless there's something more pressing like a good movie. The Bible takes a less casual view of married sex.

We understand there are hindrances to frequent sex such as aging, illness, and travel as well as many other circumstances. But the Bible gives only one reason not to have frequent sex and then only for a short time - prayer.

A special time of prayer is the only reason for a break, and then only if both the husband and wife agree to abstain from sex, "except perhaps *by agreement* for a limited time, that you may devote yourselves to prayer".

We are way too casual about sex; we can take it or leave it. If something comes up then we say that sex can wait. Life is always crowding out sex.

God's Word tells us that sex is not to be taken lightly; in other words, stop being so casual about sex. It is a big deal. If you are casual about sex in your marriage the devil notices and will "tempt you because of your lack of self-control".

In addition, Paul explains to us that any interruption of frequent sex needs to be mutually agreed upon; that is, both spouses must sign off on the abstinence from sex and then only "for a limited time".

The next time something threatens frequent sex there needs to be a conversation between you and your spouse. It could be about the next annual retreat or church conference. Paul says to talk to your spouse and come to a mutual agreement about abstaining from sex.

BIBLE THOUGHT: A married couple should make sex a

priority and talk about any potential interference in their sexual frequency.

Prayer: Father, help me understand that any break in frequent sex must be mutually agreed upon. Renew my mind according to your Word. In Jesus' name. Amen.

DAY 14 - INTOXICATION

Let your fountain be blessed,
 and rejoice in the wife of your youth,
 a lovely deer, a graceful doe.
Let her breasts fill you at all times with
 delight;
 be **intoxicated** *always in her love.*
  (Proverbs 5:18,19 ESV Emphasis added)

There is nothing more intoxicating in this life than the anticipation of sex with the one you love. The only thing better is the actual sex. Before you object, think about it. This is just like the God we love and serve. He gave us one another to enjoy and "delight" in. He established marriage to fulfill our longing for excitement, adventure, and intoxication.

Yes, God built into us a need to be "intoxicated", to

get out of the mundane and into a special place, away from it all. His idea was that this place of intoxication would be married sex, a reprieve from the numbing ordinariness of life.

We, of course, like every other gift of God, twist it, turn it, and make it into something else. We fill the need for intoxication with drink, diamonds, pizza, video games, and so much more. God says married sex is the best intoxicating experience of your life. The best things in life are free.

If you look up "intoxicated" or "drunk" in the Bible, the only good references are to sex. Those drunk with anything else, like wine, do not fare well.

You might look at our passage and say that it's only for the husband. What about the wife? The wife is to get intoxicated also, "Let him kiss me with the kisses of his mouth! For your love is better than wine;" (Song of Solomon 1:2 ESV) or "Eat, friends, drink, and be drunk with love!" (5:1b)

God wants your spouse to be the most exciting person in the world to you. We understand that "familiarity breeds contempt" and the spouse of your youth may have faded over the years. But God tells us that this does not need to be the case. The Bible tells us to be intoxicated with the wife or husband of our youth. Our intoxicating love does not need to fade.

BIBLE THOUGHT: Married sex with the spouse of your youth should continue to be intoxicating as the years go by.

. . .

PRAYER: Father, help me to overcome my familiarity with my spouse and once again become intoxicated with their love. In Jesus' name. Amen.

DAY 15 - 7 LESSONS FROM NUMBERS 25

> *While Israel lived in Shittim, the people began to whore with the daughters of Moab. These invited the people to the sacrifices of their gods, and the people ate and bowed down to their gods. So Israel yoked himself to Baal of Peor. And the anger of the Lord was kindled against Israel. (Numbers 25:1-3 ESV)*

We're reading through the Bible in a year, something we recommend for everyone. Our first passage today was Numbers 25. It paints a horrific scene where Israel commits sexual immorality with Moabite women who then lead Israel to run after the Moabite god, Baal of Peor. God in his jealousy kills 24,000 Hebrews with a plague including the guilty leaders. The plague ends when Phinehas, Aaron's grandson, drives a spear through a Hebrew man and a Midianite woman while engaged in the sex act.

Paul tells us this event is an example for us in 1 Corinthians 10 and Jesus chastises the church at Pergamum for succumbing to the same temptation as the Hebrews at Shittim in Revelation 2. Both suggest that sexual temptation is a primary strategy of the enemy and a doorway to idolatry.

What was the attraction of the Moabite women? What was wrong with the Hebrew women? The Israelite men apparently were mesmerized by the exotic cult sex of Baal of Peor. These foreign women seemed more exciting and enthusiastic than the familiar Hebrew women. The Moabite women promised exotic sexual practices the Hebrew men could not resist.

The modern application is too obvious even to mention. There is nothing new under the sun. Sexual temptation is everywhere and ready to seduce the strongest of us.

What can we learn from this event?

1. Sexual temptation is more powerful than we are.
2. Sexual temptation is one of Satan's main strategies.
3. The threat of God's punishment is not enough to keep us from sexual sin.
4. Exotic, strange sexual partners promise one thing and deliver something else.
5. Sexual sin often leads to idolatry.
6. It's probably good to run from sexual temptation.

7. Stay at home and rejoice in the wife of your youth.

Paul eases our anxiety by telling us that God has provided a way of escape from every temptation and he will not tempt us beyond our ability to resist. Whew! (See 1 Corinthians 10:13)

God has provided a way of escape from every temptation including sexual temptation.

God's Word tells us clearly that the only escape from sexual temptation is married sex, "But because of the temptation to sexual immorality, each man should have his own wife and each woman her own husband." (See 1 Corinthians 7:1-5) Occasional sex is not going to help; in fact, it may make it harder to resist. Only frequent and reciprocal married sex will make us an overcomer.

BIBLE THOUGHT: Lots of married sex is God's way of escape from sexual temptation.

PRAYER: Father, help me to overcome sexual temptation by delighting in the the spouse of my youth. In Jesus' name. Amen.

DAY 16 - THE ROYAL WEDDING

And the angel said to me, "Write this: Blessed are those who are invited to the marriage supper of the Lamb." And he said to me, "These are the true words of God." (Revelation 19:9 ESV)

The world is always captivated by a Royal wedding. It's a dazzling event filled with fanfare and celebrities. We all love weddings, admit it. Weddings fill us with hope and joy.

God loves weddings too! How do we know?

God starts the Bible with a wedding. "Therefore a man shall leave his father and his mother and hold fast to his wife, and they shall become one flesh." (Genesis 2:24)

Jesus' first miracle was at a wedding. "Jesus also was invited to the wedding with his disciples." (John 2:2) He attended and saved the day by turning water into wine.

God ends the Bible with a wedding, "The Marriage Supper of the Lamb" where the Bride, the church, will be united to the groom, Christ, forever in Heaven, "These are the true words of God." By the way, it's nice to be invited to a Royal wedding but much better to be invited to this wedding!

What is a wedding? It is the public declaration of love and the beginning of a marriage. And what makes a marriage? As we learned on **Day 1**, it is the consummation.

A wedding is a vow before the world to love another "in good times and in bad". The consummation after the wedding vows is the private declaration of love and loyalty. And sex each subsequent time in a marriage renews the wedding vows, the vows of love and loyalty.

Love is a verb. Love by definition requires action. We can say "I love you" but it means nothing until we put our words into action. Sex is the act of love in a marriage.

Taking out the garbage, mowing the lawn, taking the kids to soccer practice, doing laundry, and going on a date are all acts of love however, nothing says, "I love you" louder than sex.

Sex in marriage proves you mean it when you say "I love you". Love is not cheap. There is always a cost for love. The cost of love in marriage is setting priorities and sticking to them. Sex is the number one priority in marriage by God's very definition of marriage, "one flesh".

The public declaration of love in a wedding is made once. The private declaration of love is putting our initial vow of love into action - frequently. Sex is declaring our love over and over and over again.

God loves weddings, the ones on earth between a man and a woman, and the one in the future between Christ and his church. Everyone is invited to the one in Heaven. Have you accepted the invitation?

BIBLE THOUGHT: A wedding is a public vow of love. Sex is the action behind the vow.

PRAYER: Father, help me to remember my public declaration of love with a continual private declaration of love with my spouse. In Jesus' name. Amen.

DAY 17 - THE DEATH OF SEX

Let your fountain be blessed,
*   and rejoice in the wife of your youth,*
*   a lovely deer, a graceful doe.*
Let her breasts fill you at all times with
*   delight;*
*   be intoxicated always in her love.*
*   (Proverbs 5:15-19 ESV)*

- U.S. Marriage Rate Hits New Low and May Continue to Decline[1]
- The U.S. Fertility Rate Just Hit a Historic Low. Why Some Demographers are Freaking Out[2]
- Americans are Having Sex Less Often, New Study Shows[3]

Cyber Celibacy

There's a connection between fewer marriages, fewer babies, and less sex. We're not sociologists but you don't have to be one to see sex is heading in the wrong direction. The good news is we're still having sex, the bad news is the future of sex, as we know it, does not look bright.

In Japan, the most digitally immersed society on the planet, there is phenomenon called The Celibacy Syndrome[4] where young people are opting out of partner sex altogether and one of the reasons is the easy access to porn. The limited data is inconclusive but the decline in marriages, births, and sex are not. The government admits this could be catastrophic as the population continues to dwindle.

What's going on? We don't pretend to know fully but we suspect the further we get from the physical world the less physical we will get with each other.

Physical World

The verse above, "Let her breasts fill you *at all times* with delight" is hyperbole for the purpose of making a point. The biblical author understood the physical nature of marriage. He wanted to tell his son the only way to avoid sexual temptation - get physical with your wife. This is for husbands and wives alike.

The original audience, both husbands and wives, got the point because they lived in a physical world devoid of digital technology, social media, sedentary jobs, and the stress of modern life.

Their lives consisted of physical activities: animal

husbandry, gardening, craftsmanship, hunting and gathering for their daily sustenance. They housed their goats and sheep during the cold months in stables adjacent to their living spaces.

They witnessed the animals mating, defecating, and dying. Their loved ones died in their homes and not in a sanitized hospital. In other words, they lived in the real world, a physical world, a messy world - imperfect but gloriously physical.

They understood the physical nature of life and marriage. Life was physical, marriage was physical. They didn't Google "How to have a great sex life". They just did it.

The further we get from the real, physical world, the less physical sex becomes. Our screens become the substitute reality. Our relationships become "online" while we still live "offline".

BIBLE THOUGHT: The further we get from the physical world, the less physical we will get with each other.

PRAYER: Father, help me make our marriage more physical more often, reflecting our spiritual oneness in Christ more fully. In Jesus' name. Amen.

DAY 18 - MOSTLY DEAD SEX LIFE

I opened to my beloved,
  but my beloved had turned and gone.
My soul failed me when he spoke.
I sought him, but found him not;
  I called him, but he gave no answer.
The watchmen found me
  as they went about in the city;
they beat me, they bruised me,
  they took away my veil,
  those watchmen of the walls. (Song of
    Solomon 5:6,7 ESV)

On Day 17 we declared "The Death of Sex" as we know it. We lamented the place of sex in our new cyber society. However, today we are looking at The Death of Sex in our marriages. Sex in your marriage may look dead but it could be only *mostly* dead.

Miracle Max in "The Princess Bride" stands over an unconscious Westley and pronounces, "He is only *mostly* dead. Not *all* dead. You can bring them back to life if they are only *mostly* dead."

The same could be said of an ailing sex life: If it's not *all* dead there is hope. A *mostly* dead sex life, can be brought back to life with our desire to change and God's help. If there is any trace of passion, no matter how small, then there is always hope for more.

Trouble in Paradise

We tend to think that the lovers in the Song of Solomon experienced endless marital bliss but nothing could be further from the truth. Our lovers started off on fire but hit a dry spell not long after. Our passage is poetic in language but the author's point is clear that there will be times of sexual dryness in the best of marriages.

The beloved bride is distraught that she unintentionally rebuffed the sexual attentions of her lover. Her lover runs into the night anxious over his perceived sexual rejection. They are both angry and frustrated with the other. They have hit a dry spell with emotions overflowing into loathing for one another at the perceived slights.

Our author shows us there are consequences to sexual misunderstandings in our marriages. The beloved wife goes out into the streets looking for her lover only to be used and abused by the watchmen. The husband is nowhere to be found nursing the wounds of rejection and thinking all kinds of negative thoughts.

The good news is that they return to passion in the next chapter having found one another. They seem to have recovered from the rough patch and go on to even greater passion and love.

There are many forces opposed to frequent and reciprocal sex in marriage. There will be times when circumstances, misunderstandings, and negative emotions overwhelm our sex lives. We may loathe one another for a season but we must remember our covenant relationship in Christ and the commitment we made on our wedding day.

If there is a dry spell then ask God in prayer for reconciliation with your spouse and revived passion. God will answer your prayer.

BIBLE THOUGHT: Even the best of lovers can be derailed for a time.

PRAYER: Father, help me to understand there will be dry spells in our sex life. Help me to hope in renewal depending on you to revive us in passion as we go to you in prayer. In Jesus' name. Amen.

DAY 19 - 3 ENEMIES OF SEX

So here's what I want you to do, God helping you: Take your everyday, ordinary life — your sleeping, eating, going-to-work, and walking-around life — and place it before God as an offering. Embracing what God does for you is the best thing you can do for him. Don't become so well-adjusted to your culture that you fit into it without even thinking. Instead, fix your attention on God. You'll be changed from the inside out. Readily recognize what he wants from you, and quickly respond to it. Unlike the culture around you, always dragging you down to its level of immaturity, God brings the best out of you, develops well-formed maturity in you. (Romans 12:1,2 MSG)

The Message, a paraphrase by Eugene Peterson, captures the essence of this passage. It tells us to do ordinary life God's way. Whether sleeping, eating, or going to work, do it in a way that honors God. Don't be overly influenced by the immaturity of the culture but renew your mind, your thinking, according to God's Word.

We would say this applies to all areas of life including sex or should we say especially sex .

The goal of God's will for us is maturity in Christ. We would add that immaturity in Christ makes for a strained sex life. And before we start pointing fingers at our spouse, we need to look at ourselves first.

The opposite is also true though: Maturity in Christ; that is, the ability to understand negative cultural and religious influences, is the beginning of a mature sex life. *In other words, grow in Christ and you will experience a more satisfying sex life God's way.*

3 Enemies of Sex

Culture - Church - Character

Paul tells us to recognize the negative influences of the culture, and the church, and that will help us grow in character (or maturity). We'll summarize the three enemies today and then take a look at each in more detail on subsequent days.

Our choice is to accept the culture or accept God's Word. Sometimes the culture and the Word fit together but not very often and certainly not when it comes to sex.

Here are the enemies of sex and a quick summary of the negative influences. These influences, if embraced, will kill our sex lives, if we're not careful. In fact, we would say these wrong ideas are the leading causes of the decline in sex around the world. But that's for yet another day.

1. **Culture** - Demonization of masculinity and femininity and the movement toward gender neutrality undermines biblical married sex.
2. **Church** - Sexual restraint and false piety teach us that sex is, at best, a necessary evil and, at worse, a fleshly excess.
3. **Character** - Spiritual immaturity embraces wrong thinking about the purpose of sex in our marriages and will always lead to a less satisfying sex life.

In summary, discern the lies of the culture and religion about sex and pick up God's truth. If you do you will be conforming to God's purpose in marriage and not squeezed into the wrong thinking of the culture and church.

BIBLE THOUGHT: Don't become so well-adjusted to your culture that you fit into it without even thinking.

. . .

PRAYER: Father, help me to discern the lies of the culture, and religion, and thereby grow in maturity in Christ. In Jesus' name. Amen.

DAY 20 - PETRI DISH FOR PORN

Don't become so well-adjusted to your culture that you fit into it without even thinking. Instead, fix your attention on God. You'll be changed from the inside out. Readily recognize what he wants from you, and quickly respond to it. Unlike the culture around you, always dragging you down to its level of immaturity, God brings the best out of you, develops well-formed maturity in you. (Romans 12:2 MSG)

Part 1 - CULTURE - Demonization of Masculinity and Femininity

OUR CULTURE IS a petri dish for porn. Let us explain.

Dissing Men, Shaming Women

Men are labeled "toxic" by the culture. Men have screwed it up so now it's time for a change according to many. This logic is hard to argue with considering the horrific #MeToo stories.

However, men *and* women, have behaved badly since the Garden and are likely to continue to behave badly until they align themselves with God's purpose in marriage.

Along with dissing men, the culture shames women who "give men what they want". Women who express sensuality, no matter how slight, are considered traitors to the fight against male toxicity.

The net result of dissing men and shaming women is a move toward gender neutrality where the masculine and feminine merge into a gray-brown ideology of androgyny.

The culture projects that men and women are essentially the same and that gender distinctions are artificial, arbitrary, and a legacy of a misinformed past.

Principle of Separation

However, God "made them male and female". Same in value and worth, but distinct, especially physically, for the purpose of finding joy in the difference. God says men and women are as different as day and night and that's a good thing. Ironically, the closer we make men and women, the farther apart we become.

The creation account highlights the importance of

God's Principle of Separation: heaven and earth, light and dark, day and night, morning and evening, clouds and seas, water and dry land, and male and female. (See Genesis 1:27,28 ESV)

The difference between men and women fuels attraction and arousal in a way sameness cannot. The less unique, or the more sameness, to put it another way, the less sex and the less satisfying sex.

Paradoxically, the difference God has built into us is the foundation of a "one flesh" marriage.

God's Math

1 Male + 1 Female = 1 Flesh;

Culture's Math

1 Person + 1 Person = 2 People living life together, sharing interests and chores.

Petri Dish for Porn

When we are influenced by gender sameness, not only will our sex be less frequent and less satisfying, we will be intuitively attracted to anyone who displays the separation. The heterosexual porn industry exploits the difference and profits from it.

The perfect petri dish for porn is gender neutrality because it leaves a hunger for the difference. We're built for difference, or separation, between the sexes. When we think and look alike then attraction fades, sex fades, and marriages dry up.

Heterosexual pornography appeals to a sexuality of separation and shows us that the difference is exciting. It's no wonder there is an epidemic of porn.

. . .

DISCLAIMER

We're not saying women can't wear pants or that they should compete with porn stars! We are simply saying beware of the influence of the culture that implies men and women are essentially the same.

VIVE LA DIFFERENCE!

BIBLE THOUGHT: When we understand God's separation of the sexes and emphasize the difference in our marriages, our sex lives will take on new life.

PRAYER: Father, help me to discern the negative influences of the culture in my marriage. In Jesus' name. Amen.

DAY 21 - THE LAST TABOO

Don't become so well-adjusted to your culture that you fit into it without even thinking. Instead, fix your attention on God. You'll be changed from the inside out. Readily recognize what he wants from you, and quickly respond to it. Unlike the culture around you, always dragging you down to its level of immaturity, God brings the best out of you, develops well-formed maturity in you. (Romans 12:2 MSG)

---

*P*art 2 - CHURCH - Sexual Restraint and the Modesty Movement

THE LAST TABOO of the church is sex. We've overcome

a lot of religion over the years but the denial, obfuscation, and misunderstanding of sex in the church continues. Our books are for the sole purpose of bringing sex out from under the bushel of religion and into the glorious light of the gospel.

Christian Sub-Culture

Christian gnosticism (aka docetism) exalts the spiritual over the physical. This dangerous Christian sub-culture teaches sexual restraint for men and false piety for women as the way of holiness in marriage. God thinks differently. Lots of sex with our spouse contributes to our holiness not self restraint.

Paul says, "Don't become so well-adjusted to your culture that you fit into it without even thinking." This includes the Christian sub-culture that represses married sex.

God is for married sex. He loves sex. God created sex and thinks it's pretty cool. God uses it to describe the intimacy between Christ and his church. He even declared it, as part of his creation, "Very Good". (See Genesis 1:31 ESV)

Modesty

The Christian idea of false modesty, in the name of saving our brothers in Christ from falling into sexual sin, has taken a left turn. This is nothing less than religion; that is, trying to impress God with *our* "holiness".

Incredibly, Christian modesty promotes the cultural

trend of gender neutrality. We have taken on the uniform of sexual sameness in the name of "holiness".

There are two problems with excessive modesty. The first is the false idea that we are helping our brothers in Christ avoid sexual sin. This is, at best, false optimism and, at worse, spiritual pride. Immature men will fall whether you dress modestly or not.

The second, and most insidious problem, is when modesty becomes a way of life, when our identity is tied to it. Wrong thinking about modesty will lead to a suppression of sensuality in the marriage bed. A casual reading of the *Song of Songs* reveals that this is not God's intention for the marriage bed.

Be modest, of course, but be careful that it's not an excuse to avoid sensuality. It's hard to shift gears from a pious, modest, asexual Christian in church to an enthusiastic, reciprocal sex partner in the bedroom.

BIBLE THOUGHT: Religion tries to impress God with sexual restraint in marriage. God has a better way.

PRAYER: Father, help me to realize that my righteousness is in Christ alone and not in my performance. In Jesus' name. Amen.

DAY 22 - LOVING THE UNLOVABLE LOVER

Love is patient and kind; love does not envy or boast; it is not arrogant or rude. It does not insist on its own way; it is not irritable or resentful; it does not rejoice at wrongdoing, but rejoices with the truth. Love bears all things, believes all things, hopes all things, endures all things. Love never ends. (1 Corinthians 13:4-8a ESV)

Part 3 - CHARACTER - Immaturity embraces wrong thinking

THERE ARE **3 Enemies of Sex**

The first enemy is absorbing any negative cultural influences that undermine sex. The second is picking up sex-killing religious attitudes from the church. And the third is spiritual and emotional immaturity of either spouse.

Any one of these can kill sex in the best of marriages, and if one or the other spouse, or both, have all three then the end is near. However, we all entered marriage relatively immature, emotionally and spiritually, especially if we married young. There is hope.

God wants us to mature in Christ, discern the negative influences of the culture, and have a sex-positive attitude. This is not done overnight. It takes time and patience but it is possible with God.

The Immature Lover

What does an immature lover look like? Well, they exhibit the opposite of the loving attributes in our passage today. An immature lover is impatient, insists on their own way, gives up when the going gets tough, and is often irritable and resentful about sex.

It's hard to have sex with this person. However, we were this person at one time - or some iteration of them. Maturity is growing, not arriving. Be patient and kind.

The Mature Lover

What does a mature lover look like? Everything on our list plus the capacity to love the immature lover. This capacity to love the unlovable lover comes from outside ourselves. The Fruit of the Spirit, love, is a by-product of growing in the grace and knowledge of Jesus Christ. (See 2 Peter 3:18)

If you married an immature person, and we were all somewhere on the spectrum of immaturity when we married, don't withhold sex because they are immature but pray for their maturity.

Also, treat your spouse as if they were mature; that is, extend grace to your unlovable lover just as Christ extends grace to us every day, a sinner in need of grace.

We have sex with the unlovable lover primarily because we promised to have sex with them the day we got married. A mature person understands the covenant commitment of marriage.

What's love got to do with it? Everything. However, if things get to the point where bitterness and resentment overwhelm you then seek help from your pastor or a professional Christian counselor. Sometimes it takes extreme grace *and* extreme action to keep a marriage together.

Fight for your marriage.

BIBLE THOUGHT: Maturity is extending grace and withholding condemnation.

PRAYER: Father, help me to pick up my conjugal responsibilities and lay down any resentment or bitterness toward my spouse. In Jesus' name. Amen.

DAY 23 - THERE'S MORE TO LIFE THAN SEX!

> ***You shall not commit adultery.** (Exodus 20:14)*
> ***You shall not covet your neighbor's wife.** (Exodus 20:17)*
> ***Abstain from ... sexual immorality.** (Acts 15:29)*

We know a lot of you want to know what the Bible says about sex and that's why you're reading our devotional. Good for you and thank you!

You may also be thinking that there's more to life than sex! Why do we obsess over sex? We may seem to give it a bigger place than it deserves. After all, sex is just one of many elements of life and marriage.

Good point. Let's take a look at what God thinks.

. . .

THREE SIGNIFICANT EPOCHS in the Story of God

God gives his people specific instructions in Scriptures. He doesn't want to leave any room for doubt. There are three important sets of instructions at significant points in the story of his people: The Law, The New Covenant, and The Last Days.

The first set of instructions is the famous one, The Ten Commandments, given at the beginning of The Law. The second set of instructions is at the beginning of the church for Gentiles at the Council at Jerusalem. The third set of instructions is given to the seven churches at the beginning of Revelation in the Last Days.

Sex is a big part of each set of instructions. If God makes a big deal out of sex who are we to argue?

THE MATH

Two of the Ten Commandments concern sex. If you eliminate the four vertical commandments (our relationship with God), you're left with two of the six horizontal commandments (our relationship with each other) addressing sex. 33% of God's instructions in the Ten Commandments is about sex: "You shall not commit adultery" and "You shall not covet your neighbor's wife." (Exodus 20:14,17 ESV)

The Council at Jerusalem seemed confused that God would allow Gentiles into the Kingdom but once they got over their initial shock they issued four instructions to the new gentile believers: "That you abstain from what has been sacrificed to idols, and from blood, and from what has been strangled, and from sexual immorality." (Acts 15:29) We could lump the first three together as "eating rules" and then sexual immorality as as separate category making it 50% of the instructions.

The third set is the instructions to the seven churches in Revelation. Two of the seven churches, Pergamum and Thyatira, are chastised for allowing sexual immorality in their midst. The math calculates to 28%.

God's Big Three set of instructions include anywhere from 25% to 50% of instructions to avoid sexual immorality. On average, nearly a third of God's instructions concern overcoming sexual sin. God thinks sex; that is, overcoming sexual sin, is a very big part of life any way you do the math.

And what is God's only solution to sexual immorality? The short answer is frequent and reciprocal sex with your spouse!

BIBLE THOUGHT: God thinks sex is big deal and so should we.

PRAYER: Father, you created sex. Help me to put it in proper perspective for my good and your glory. In Jesus' name. Amen.

DAY 24 - HAVE SEX TO FORGET ABOUT SEX

Put to death therefore what is earthly in you: sexual immorality, impurity, passion, evil desire, and covetousness, which is idolatry. (Colossians 3:5 ESV)

John Piper says that idolatry today is not usually worshipping a carved image but rather it is an activity of the human heart. It's essentially craving something more than God. Anything, but more often than not, usually some comfort like food, wine, exercise, recognition, or sex.

One way we can know we have an idol is by examining our thoughts. What do we think about the most? What do we want the most? If it's anything more than God's grace, it could be an idol. God is a jealous God and wants our attention.

. . .

Comfort Calls Our Name

Comfort permeates the Colossians passage above, "Sexual immorality, impurity, passion, evil desire, and covetousness". Sex certainly comes to mind when we read this passage but it could be anything from craving the best garden in the neighborhood to lusting after a pepperoni pizza night after night.

Human beings, men and women, have a lust problem. Lust is an inordinate craving. It could be sex or food, and the lusting can come and go, but usually there's a pattern of obsession in us that repeats itself over and over.

Sex quickly becomes an idol if we haven't had sex in a while and there is no prospect for sex in the near future.

Our passage says clearly that sexual immorality is idolatry. Paul tells us to "put it to death".

How do we "put to death" sexual immorality? God's Word in 1 Corinthians 7:1-5 tells us the *only* way to put to death sexual immorality - get married and have lots of sex.

Sex quickly becomes an idol if we haven't had sex in a while and there is no prospect for sex in the near future. God created us with a very strong sex drive, men and women, and he has made a provision to overcome our strong sex drive. He doesn't leave us on our own. He provides a way. The way is a sex-soaked marriage.

When we have had sex recently and know we will have sex soon then sexual tension dissipates and then sex is then less likely to become an idol.

. . .

HAVE Sex to Forget about Sex

Frequent and reciprocal sex with your spouse puts sex in it's proper place in our life.

If our sexual desires are fulfilled, we won't be constantly thinking about it. God tells us to have sex frequently so we won't be overcome and lose self-control. (See 1 Corinthians 7:5)

Have sex to forget about sex so that you can move on with the rest of your life.

BIBLE THOUGHT: Sex can become an idol when we don't have frequent and reciprocal sex with our spouse.

PRAYER: Father, help me from making sex an idol. Show me the many benefits of sex with my spouse including staying away from idolatry. In Jesus' name. Amen.

DAY 25 - PAY ATTENTION

*I am my beloved's,
and his desire is for me.
(Song of Solomon 7:10 ESV)*

---

*G*od is a jealous God and wants our attention. He doesn't demand our attention although he is the only one worthy of our attention. He is altogether lovely, his excellencies are unlimited, his beauty is fathomless, and he is the only one worthy of our first and best attention.

We have free will so he doesn't demand our attention but it would do us well to give him the attention he deserves. It is for our benefit; after all, he doesn't need our attention but knows it is the best thing we can do for ourselves.

God notices when we give him attention in worship

and prayer in faith. Our attention turns to affection as we see him for who he is even in our limited capacity to comprehended his infinite love. Similarly, your spouse deserves your attention and should expect your attention.

Your Spouse is **Jealous**

Your spouse has every right to be jealous of anything you pay attention to more than them. When you got married, you promised your spouse that they would be the most important thing in your life and your primary concern.

Pauls tells husbands, after giving God the attention he deserves, the best thing you can do for yourself is give your wife your full attention and affection. After all, you pamper yourself, so pamper your wife! It's actually the same thing.

> *In the same way husbands should love their wives as their own bodies. He who loves his wife loves himself. (Ephesians 5:28,29)*

When a husband's attention is divided, his wife will feel less valued than whatever gets most of his attention. Most of us have jobs to go to, activities we enjoy, and duties to perform but your wife should feel she is the greatest treasure in your life and your first priority.

Likewise the wife should make her husband feel he is the most important person besides Christ in her life. When this full attention is flowing both ways then you have the foundations of a healthy marriage. Give one another the attention they deserve, and promised when you got married. Divided attention, divides marriages.

ATTENTION ALWAYS LEADS to Affection

Our *Song of Solomon* passage paints the picture of a satisfied wife, one who knows that her husband desires her more than anything in this world. "I am my beloved's, and his desire is for me." She is confident in his undivided attention. She knows that she is his first priority because she receives his full attention. She responds to his attention with the gift of her affection.

Of course, we're talking about the proper kind of attention! We're talking about positive attention. The kind of attention Solomon gives his bride in our passage although any positive attention is good attention.

Positive attention leads to positive affection. An all too common storyline is the neglected spouse who receives attention from a co-worker. Affair-proof your marriage by giving your spouse the attention you promised when you got married. A neglected spouse is an affair waiting to happen. There are many reasons you can't control that lead to a failed marriage but attention is not one of them.

Pay attention.

BIBLE THOUGHT: Attention always leads to affection.

PRAYER: Father, help me to value, respect and put my spouse first after you. In Jesus' name. Amen.

DAY 26 - GET UNCOMFORTABLE

And I will lead the blind
in a way that they do not know,
in paths that they have not known
I will guide them.
I will turn the darkness before them
    into light,
the rough places into level ground.
These are the things I do,
and I do not forsake them. (Isaiah
    42:16 ESV)

Technology is daunting when we first encounter it. Perhaps you had to learn a new software program for your job. We remember our companies preparing us for months in advance for new software. Everyone was in a panic but once it rolled out, and we got used to it, we never gave it a second thought.

Changing our sexual habits is daunting. We've grown accustomed to our sexual patterns like an old pair of slippers. It's safe and comfortable. We have unspoken rules about sex, frequency and reciprocity, in our marriage. So when we understand God's Word has specific directives for married sex, we tend to deny or ignore them. We fall back on our cultural and religious preconceptions about married sex.

A Disciple of Jesus Expects & Embraces Change

However, being a disciple of Jesus, we know, requires constant reassessment of our habits and patterns. Jesus always calls us out of our comfort zones and into uncomfortable places such as witnessing to our neighbors, feeding the hungry at the homeless shelter, or giving up a long time habit. It's the same with our marriage and especially our sex lives.

When we understand God's Word and realize we have to change, it takes us by surprise. But as a disciple we desire to do life God's way and know there's always good in obedience. "Whoever gives thought to the word will discover good, and blessed is he who trusts in the Lord." (Proverbs 16:20) We want to have a marriage that reflects the Word even if it's uncomfortable.

Changing our sexual patterns can be uncomfortable for many reasons but we are called to overcome all obstacles and get out of our comfort zones. There is a cost to following Jesus and marriage God's way is no exception. Jesus calls us to a place of humility, surrender, and love in marriage and that means frequent and reciprocal sex. (See The Principles of Marriage ESV)

. . .

PRINCIPLES OF MARRIAGE

God wants us to understand the Principles of Marriage and practice them regularly. It requires us to get out of our comfort zones and into God's place of obedience. The good news is that he will guide us and "turn the darkness before (us) into light, the rough places into level ground." The Holy Spirit will comfort us when we get uncomfortable in the places he sends us. Trust him.

BIBLE THOUGHT: God wants us to get uncomfortable for our good and his glory.

PRAYER: Father, help me to get out of my usual areas of comfort. Help me to put my spouse first even when it's uncomfortable. In Jesus' name. Amen.

DAY 27 - SATAN'S WISH LIST

Do not deprive one another, except perhaps by agreement for a limited time, that you may devote yourselves to prayer; but then come together again, so that Satan may not tempt you because of your lack of self-control. *(1 Corinthians 7:5 ESV emphasis added)*

---

*S*ometimes it seems no one believes in the devil anymore. He has become a cartoon character. Jesus talked a lot about Satan, so we're going with Jesus on this one.

And lead us not into temptation, but deliver us from the evil one. (Matthew 6:13 NIV)

SATAN DOES NOT WANT You to Have Sex with Your Spouse

The number one goal of Satan is to keep husbands and wives from having sex. We're not saying this, Paul is saying this. God's Word tells us clearly in our passage that Satan looks forward to you not having sex with your spouse. In fact, he loves it when you have infrequent and non-reciprocal sex because he knows you are then ripe for sexual sin, *"so that Satan may not tempt you because of your lack of self-control."*

Satan will do anything he can to keep you from having sex so that you will lose "self-control". He loves it when you are out of control sexually. He looks for opportunities to strike when he senses your sexual and emotional needs are not being met. This can lead to physical or emotional affairs with someone other than your spouse.

SATAN WILL DISTRACT You from Sex in Three Ways

1. Circumstances - He will encourage a lifestyle that is so crammed with places to go and things to do that there's just no time for sex.
2. Distraction - He will tell you that everything is more important than sex. If you think sex is the next thing on the agenda then he will introduce an urgent need to distract you.

3. Deception - He will try to convince you that frequent sex with your spouse is excessive sensuality and that you need to stuff it to show "real" self-control. He will also try to convince your spouse that sex with you is the last thing they want or need.

God's Word, on the other hand, tells us that frequent and reciprocal sex is the way to counter Satan's temptations. Paul reminds us that sex is one of Satan's favorite temptations. We would say that it's in the top 3 right after pride and power although an argument could be made for it being number one on Satan's list for marriages.

Counterattack

How do we fight back against the attacks of the evil one? First, "do not deprive one another" in other words: Just do it. Second, realize your life is busy so you need to make room for sex. Thirdly, do not be unaware of Satan's schemes to thwart sex. And finally, stand against the lies of the devil by reading and re-reading God's Word especially 1 Corinthians 7:1-5 and The Song of Solomon.

Fight for your right to have sex, resist the devil, and he will flee. Don't be taken in by the lies of the evil one who is prowling about like a lion seeking whom he may devour with sexual temptation.

. . .

BIBLE THOUGHT: Satan loves it when you don't have frequent and reciprocal sex with your spouse.

PRAYER: Father, help me be aware of Satan's attempts to deceive me and fill my mind with lies. Help me to stand on your Word of Truth about married sex. In Jesus' name. Amen.

DAY 28 - LIFE IS SHORT

Why, you do not even know what will happen tomorrow. What is your life? You are a mist that appears for a little while and then vanishes. (James 4:14 NIV)

Most people at the end of their life don't say that they should have worked more, traveled less, or made love fewer times.

Life is short and God wants us to major on the major and minor the minor and not get distracted from what's really important. We get messed up and our thinking gets skewed as we go merrily along in life. As we learned, Satan's task is to get us off course and confuse us about what is really important.

The entire Bible is about getting our priorities straight when you really think about it. Every time we take up the Word the Holy Spirit is trying to break through our prejudices and preconceptions about life. He is trying to shock us into reality. He says, "Hey, wake up! The Word is true. Stop doing what you're doing. Do life God's way because he loves you and knows what's best for you."

> *"Wake up, sleeper,*
> *rise from the dead,*
> *and Christ will shine on you." (Ephesians 5:14)*

What does it mean to "Wake up, rise from the dead"? It means that we should see the world through the eyes of the Word and then respond appropriately. When you "wake up" to the instruction of the Holy Spirit then "Christ will shine on you". It seems to us that's a good thing.

In marriage, Christ's light shining on us produces love and intimacy reflecting his love and intimacy for his people. It is to see our spouse as our most important relationship outside of Christ. It's to work at our relationship with humility, forgiveness, and hope.

> *"For this reason a man will leave his father*
> *and mother and be united to his wife,*
> *and the two will become one flesh." This*
> *is a profound mystery but I am talking*
> *about Christ and the church. (Ephesians 5:31,32)*

When we get to the end to our life, we will not say we

made love too many times with our spouse. Don't let the locust eat up the years of your youth with unimportant stuff. It took us many years (40!) to discover God's truth about intimacy in marriage.

The purpose of our books is to help you discover this truth a lot sooner than we did. May Christ's light shine on you in your marriage!

Bible Thought: Marriage is important to God because it is the essential building block of a peaceful, productive society and a reflection of Christ and his church.

Prayer: Father, help me to live my life to the fullest according to your Word. Help me love and respect my spouse. In Jesus' name. Amen.

DAY 29 - MARRIAGE: GOD'S BOOT CAMP

The Song of Songs, which is Solomon's.
(Song of Solomon 1:1 ESV)

We're going to tackle *The Song of Solomon* today since it celebrates sexual love between a husband and wife. It also is a picture of Christ and his church echoing Ephesians 5:31,32. These are not contradictory because God himself chooses to compare marital love with Christ's love for his bride, the church.

In our church culture, we often separate the physical and spiritual, lifting the spiritual above the physical. God wants us to be comfortable with both the spiritual and physical realities of his creation and see them the way he sees them. To this end, he gives us *The Song of Solomon* as his picture of ideal married love.

If he wanted only a spiritual universe occupied by spiritual beings then he had that with the angels before

Creation. But he wanted something physical, lavish, and sensual so he created the earth with Adam and Eve at the center, declaring them "one flesh" in marriage.

The Best of the Best

The author starts with the words, "Song of Songs" in verse 1. It's like saying "the best of the best". The writer is declaring that this song is the highest song of all songs, there is no higher or more important song in all the world. This is the *Song of Songs* of Solomon; that is, this *Song* is the highest and best of all his writings. That's is saying something!

Our author is not contradicting God's supreme position, he is simply saying that the sexual relationship God intended between a husband and wife is the highest, most glorious, relationship in all of God's creation outside of our relationship with God himself.

Love One Another

Jesus says, "By this everyone will know that you are my disciples, if you love one another." (John 13:35 NIV) Jesus tells us, on more than one occasion, that love is the goal of the Christian life. We can know the Bible, prophesy, perform signs and wonders, but only love counts in the end. Love is the Fruit of the Spirit and flows from a close personal relationship with Christ.

If we can't love our spouse then how can we love God or anyone else? In fact, marriage is God's boot camp for learning how to love another person. Let's start with a sincere, gospel-centered, God-honoring love of our spouse and then we will know how to love others.

The Song of Solomon shows us exactly what a gospel-centered marriage looks like with mutual sexual submission at its core.

BIBLE THOUGHT: Marriage is God's Boot Camp of love.

PRAYER: Father, help me to learn how to love my spouse so I can be used by you to show love to the rest of the world. In Jesus' name. Amen.

DAY 30 - HOW TO BE SEX-POSITIVE

The Song of Songs, which is Solomon's.
She
Let him kiss me with the kisses of his
   mouth! (Song of Solomon 1:1,2a ESV)

The Song of Songs is a love poem extolling the joy of sexual intimacy in marriage. God wants us to consider it as a picture of an ideal marriage. It is no accident God included this curious book in his canon of Scripture.

We call it curious because many Christian don't want to think about sex, let alone talk about it. God has other ideas and lets us know by putting a book all about sexual intimacy in his Word. The reality is that Satan wants us to think about sex in his terms of depravity and vulgarity.

The culture of the Middle East at the time of the

writing of the Song of Songs was sex-positive. God wants us to think about sex his way as the glorious center of a covenant marriage.

Sex Gets a Bad Rep

Sex started to get a bad reputation at the beginning of the church age. A few early church fathers went so far as to castrate themselves in the name of holiness. This was the beginning of a love-hate affair with sex in the Christian community.

Satan has taken advantage of fanatical Christian sexual ideology ever since. It's not a coincidence that the number one most vulgar word in our culture is a description of the sex act. Satan, the god of this world, wants anything God holds in esteem to be denigrated. Sexual intimacy is no exception; in fact, the devil majors on polluting what God has declared as "very good".

It's also no coincidence that the second most used profanity in our culture is our Savior's name. It's almost as if Satan says, "Yes, one day every knee will bow to the name of Jesus, but in the meantime it will be a curse word." The two most used profanities concern sexual intimacy and our Lord's name. No surprises from the god of this world.

It should tell us something about Satan's strategies to pollute our sexual intimacy in marriage and our spiritual intimacy in Christ.

Taking a Stand

So when we are, at best, ambiguous about sexual intimacy; and, at worse, repulsed by sexual intimacy then we are aligning ourselves with the devil's doctrines of polluted sex. It's only when we think correctly about married sex will we be able to do married sex as God intended.

The Song of Songs is sex-positive because God is sex-positive. It's time we take back the territory that Satan has stolen from us for 2,000 years. Married sex is God's idea and he thinks it's a good one.

BIBLE THOUGHT: God's Word celebrates sex in a committed covenant marriage.

PRAYER: Father, help me be sex-positive as God is sex-positive and stand against the cultural lies of the evil one. In Jesus' name. Amen.

DAY 31 - ATTITUDE IS EVERYTHING

The Song of Songs, which is Solomon's.
She
Let him kiss me with the kisses of his
mouth! (Song of Solomon 1:1,2a ESV)

The first thing we notice in this love poem is the wife's enthusiasm for her husband. She is on fire for his love! She can't seem to contain her excitement for his perfect kisses, "Let him kiss me with the kisses of his mouth!". Her attitude springs from sex-positive thoughts about her husband.

Attitude is Everything

William James, the 19th century American philosopher stated, "The greatest discovery of my generation is that a human being can alter his life by altering his attitudes." Attitude is everything. As Christians, we can state with confidence that the closer our attitudes align with God's attitudes the more joyful we will be in this life. In fact, our attitude significantly contributes to our happiness in this life. Let's take on God's attitude about everything especially marital intimacy.

If your attitude is sex-positive then you're on your way to enjoying sexual intimacy, and if your spouse's attitude is sex-positive, then you both can celebrate God's gift of sex equally. However, if your attitude, or your spouse's attitude, is otherwise then there's a lot of work to do. But it's worth the effort to align your attitude with God's attitude.

3 Sex-Positive Attitudes

Three things stand out to us in this passage:

1. She is the aggressor. This woman is no wilting flower waiting for her husband to make the first move. She knows her joy is in the arms of her husband and she is determined to make it happen - the sooner the better.
2. She is enthusiastic. Our protagonist is so excited about his kisses she doesn't seem to care what people might think as she declares before the world that her lover is a good kisser.
3. She is thankful. She seems extremely thankful for her husband. She is confident that her husband wants to reciprocate her affection.

She isn't afraid of his rejection; in fact, it apparently never enters her mind.

THE REALITY

This love poem, and poetry in general, uses figurative language to express emotion, truth, and beauty. The Song of Songs paints us a picture of an ideal biblical marriage. We will see later in the poem that everything is not bliss. Our lovers have a Big Misunderstanding in chapter 5 and have to overcome a common marital misconception about sex. Don't worry, we will get to this reality of married life, but for now let's enjoy the enthusiasm of the bride and smile that she loves to kiss.

Do you love to kiss? Change your attitude about kissing and see how kissing is better than you remembered. Go ahead, try it :-)

BIBLE THOUGHT: God's Word celebrates sexual intimacy, including great kissing.

PRAYER: Father, help me to change my attitude toward kissing and align myself with God's attitude toward sexual intimacy. In Jesus' name. Amen.

DAY 32 - MEN AND WOMEN ARE DIFFERENT

Let him kiss me with the kisses of
  his mouth!
For your love is better than wine;
your anointing oils are fragrant;
your name is oil poured out;
therefore virgins love you.
Draw me after you; let us run.
The king has brought me into his chambers.
  (Song of Solomon 1:2-4a ESV)

The world says that men and women are essentially the same and that women can do anything a man can do - only better. This may or may not be true but when it comes to sexual desire and perspective the Bible tells us that men and women are different.

Husband, this may come as news to you, but your wife does not think about sex the same way you do. And the more you try to get her to think about sex the way you do, well, let's just say it won't help. And wife, your husband does not think about sex the way you do either.

For example, in Proverbs we get a man's perspective, "Let her breasts fill you at all times with delight; be intoxicated always in her love." (Proverbs 5:19b). This verse encourages sexual intoxication and desire in a husband. God has gifted men with an indiscriminately strong sex drive. Now hopefully social pressures, and for the Christian man, the Holy Spirit, mitigate their wild sexual desires or they may end up in another #MeToo story.

The Difference

These two verses, Proverbs 5:19b and Song of Songs 1:1-4, give us insight into the different perspective of sex and desire between men and women. Notice both find sex intoxicating but the man is drunk with desire while the woman is intoxicated with being desired, "For your love is better than wine". She reinforces this idea of being intoxicated with being deeply desired:

"Let him kiss me with the kisses of his mouth"
"Draw me after you, let us run"
"The king has brought me into his chambers".

She is intoxicated with the intoxicating passion of her lover and his intense desire for her and her alone. This is not to say she doesn't also feel strong sexual feelings but she looks at the relationship from a different point of view.

They both love sexual intimacy but the man is overcome with desire while the woman is overcome with being desired. But the goal is the same. The path is different. God created man and woman, husband and wife, to complement one another - desire and being desired. There may be the occasional overlap and reversal in a marriage from time to time, but generally, men and women differ on sexual desire and perspective.

A Complicated Sexual Dance

Of course, we are looking at a young couple where the passion is rich and unreserved. One thing to keep in mind though is that as a marriage matures, the sexual desires seems to merge; that is, the differences are less pronounced. We think particularly of Sarah who laughed at the prospect of sexual "pleasure" at her advanced age of 90 or so. (See Genesis 18:12)

Marriage is a complicated sexual dance and the longer a marriage goes on the greater chance of a misstep. We suspect one of the major problems in a lack of sexual desire is unforgiveness. Unforgiveness leads to resentment and bitterness and the death of desire or being desired. Sexual intimacy is complicated enough without adding unforgiveness. Beware of missteps. Forgive quickly.

The Ideal Marriage

However, our young bride is living the ideal marriage in our love poem. She delights in being desired and values her lover supremely. She can't wait to consummate their relationship and delights in her husband's passion for her. As her marriage progresses we would encourage her to beware of snares and obstacles along the way that could get in the way of sexual desire. But for now she is enraptured with passion and waiting for her lover's kisses.

BIBLE THOUGHT: Beware of snares and obstacles that could undermine desire and being desired. Forgive quickly.

PRAYER: Father, help me to understand the view my spouse has of sexual intimacy. Help me to remove all obstacles that would hinder sexual intimacy in our marriage. In Jesus' name. Amen.

DAY 33 - DILUTED SENSES

*Let him kiss me with the kisses of
   his mouth!
For your love is better than wine;
your anointing oils are fragrant;
your name is oil poured out;
therefore virgins love you.
Draw me after you; let us run.
The king has brought me into his chambers.*
   (Song of Solomon 1:2-4a ESV)

As we write this, we are on vacation visiting family in northern Idaho. We're at a cabin in the country near a lake and an evergreen forest. The cabin has no Internet, cel reception, or cable. We have to drive to the local library 10 miles for WiFi to catch up on our email, texts, blog statistics, and the latest Yankees' game.

It's a big adjustment for these city folk!

We sit on the patio each morning. We taste the coffee, see the rabbits at play, feel the sunshine, hear the birds chirping, smell the the pine forest, and hold hands. All our senses are at work taking in all of God's goodness to us. God intended our senses to experience the glory of his creation and to give thanks to him for his incredible gift of the five senses.

Our Five Senses

We have, to varying degrees, exchanged the richness of our God-given senses for the counterfeit in our postmodern, digital world. Of course, we can't get away from our senses altogether but a large part of our experience is screen-centric - smartphones, flat screen TVs, and streaming music services.

There is a movement to get back to an analog life but it's like spitting in the ocean. The net result of our cool digital life is that we lose the ability to feel, truly feel, the way God designed us to feel with our five senses.

Our five senses are most alive in the act of love making, nothing is as rich or as satisfying to the senses. You may say a fine wine, an ocean sunset, a Mozart concerto are the most satisfying stimuli to our senses. God says making love to your spouse is the most satisfying stimuli to all your senses. Is there anything on this planet that engages all five senses, in the same way, at the same time, than the act of marital love? Not really. Sight, hearing, smell, touch, and taste come alive in sex unlike anything else.

. . .

Solomon and His Bride Got It

Our passage today isn't even talking about the act yet, our lovers are still in the preparation phase and all the senses are already fully engaged. The handsome king (sight), the kisses of his mouth (touch), his fragrant oil (smell), speaking his name is like "oil poured out" (hearing), and a love that is better than wine (taste).

Our five senses are a gift from God. Why did he give us this marvelous gift? Because when we are fully immersed in one or more of the senses that is when we feel most alive. God wants us to feel alive to the fullest. Jesus calls this the "abundant life". (See John 10:10)

When we get immersed in our various "screens" to satisfy only what our God-given senses can satisfy, we dilute the experience of life and feel less than truly alive. We exchange true life for a postmodern dullness. We dilute the senses to our harm. Pornography is perhaps the most diluting form of all digital dullness.

Feel Truly Alive

God has given most of us a wonderful ability to truly feel alive through our natural senses. Drink fine wine, go to the ocean and see a wonderful sunset, hike in the mountains and hear the sounds of nature but there's nothing that engages all the senses, at the same time, in the same way, like making love.

The irony that you're probably reading this post on your smartphone has not escaped us. So put the phone down, step back and take a walk in the woods or better yet find your husband or wife and give them a big kiss!

• • •

BIBLE THOUGHT: God has given us a wonderful ability to truly feel alive through our five senses.

PRAYER: Father, help me to understand the wonderful gift of the five senses and give you thanks for these glorious gifts. In Jesus' name. Amen.

DAY 34 - LASTING LOVE MUST BE TAUGHT

All Scripture is inspired by God and is useful to teach us what is true and to make us realize what is wrong in our lives. It corrects us when we are wrong and teaches us to do what is right. (2 Timothy 3:16 NLT)

You don't have to teach your child ingratitude. It comes naturally. For the most part, children must be taught what is personally good and socially appropriate. It does not come naturally.

One of the things we don't need to be taught is falling in love and, for that matter, falling out of love. Many of us fell in love and got married and then promptly fell out of love. Falling in and out of love is natural. Natural is good for food but not for a marriage.

Staying in love, on the other hand, needs to be taught. It does not come naturally.

GOD'S WORD **Teaches**

Fortunately, God understands that teaching is critical to a useful life and a fulfilling marriage. "All Scripture is inspired by God and is useful to teach us what is true."

Today the Bible is under attack as out of date, too hard to understand, and a religious idol - and this is by the church. Many, outside the church, simply discount the Bible as irrelevant.

Many years ago as a new believer, I (Rene) attended a retreat center where the retreat leader quoted me the verse below after listening to me moan about my life.

> *Whoever loves discipline loves knowledge,*
> *but whoever hates correction is stupid. (Proverbs*
> *12:1 NIV)*

He didn't say anything else and got up and left the room. I was stunned. Did he just call me "stupid"? It took me a while to get passed my hurt feelings but I knew he was right. The retreat leader's rebuke had a profound impact on me. It taught me God's Word has a way to get to the heart of a matter and that it is very practical. (See Hebrews 4:12)

One way to look at the Bible is as a book of advice - from God. God's advice to me was to humble myself and be open to align my life with his Word. He suggested a good starting point would be to stop moaning.

• • •

The Secret of Lasting Love

You don't have to teach how to fall out of love in a marriage. It comes naturally. Resentment, bitterness, and isolation are the natural byproducts of a marriage between two sinners. God knows this and that's why he has given us very specific instructions in the Bible to combat these natural tendencies.

First, he shows us our need for Jesus and the gospel of grace where we don't rely on what we do but on what Christ has done for us. Secondly, he gives us the Holy Spirit to teach us his ways, and teachers in the Body to illuminate the Scriptures. And lastly, he gives us the will and the power to follow his teachings. (See Hebrews 10:14; Hebrews 8:10-12; Ephesians 4:11)

God addresses marriage and the secret of a lasting love in 1 Corinthians 7:1-5 as well as many other passages in the Bible. In summary, 1 Corinthians 7:1-5 instructs us how we fall in love, and more importantly, how we stay in love.

Verse 2 says that we fall in love lustfully and verse 5 says that we stay in love intentionally.

The pivotal verse is the third, "The husband should give to his wife her conjugal rights, and likewise the wife to her husband." God's teaching about what makes a long and satisfying marriage pivots on conjugal rights and responsibilities of each spouse.

Yes, there's more to marriage than sex but God tells us that sex is the barometer of the health of a marriage.

Bible Thought: The Bible teaches us how to stay in love.

PRAYER: Father, I need your help every day. Show me that your Word is true and trustworthy. Teach me your ways and lead me into your abundant life. In Jesus' name. Amen.

DAY 35 - HOW TO TALK ABOUT YOU KNOW WHAT

The husband should give to his wife her conjugal rights, and likewise the wife to her husband. (1 Corinthians 7:3 ESV)

This entry is a little different than the others. Our devotional is exclusively about what the Bible says about married sex. But as we're talking more and more about our devotional to people we realize that couples simply aren't talking about sex in their marriage - at all! This is alarming to us so we thought we would suggest a few questions to get the conversation started. Chances are that if you're not talking about sex, you're not doing it very often either.

There are many reasons why married couples don't talk about sex.

We imagine for the wife it's an uncomfortable topic of conversation because they either know, or suspect, their husbands want more sex than they're getting. They'd rather not take the blame for the infrequency - again. This causes angst and guilt which leads to feeling badly about themselves or their husband or both.

Also, women, especially in our Christian culture, have been taught since childhood that sex is bad before marriage and the implication is that it's not much better after marriage. In addition, past conversations with their husbands about sex never ended well and this adds to the reluctance to talk. But for whatever reason there seems to be a loud silence in many Christian marriages.

The fact that the most intimate relationship there is in life, wife and husband, can't talk about their most intimate time together is sad. Heartbreaking really.

We imagine for the husband, he knows that he'll either come across as oversexed or worse, a predator, always demanding sex. For the Christian man, this also reveals how unspiritual he is being concerned about the things of the "flesh". And we all know the flesh is evil; therefore, sex becomes a "necessary evil".

What Makes a Successful Marriage - Pew Report

It's a shame that more wives and husbands don't talk about sex. In a recent Pew survey, the number one reason to get married was "love" (88%). When Pew Research Center asked what makes a successful marriage, a close second to "shared interests" (64%), was a "satisfying sex life" (61%). This suggests that we get married for love and then after we're married for a while we realize that a "satisfying sex life" is one of the major reasons we stay together.

As we said, there are many reasons including past abuse and promiscuity as reasons not to talk about sex. Sex is an uncomfortable topic and it can get emotional quickly. However, we believe that it's worth the risk.

Below are five open-ended, non-threatening (mostly), questions that are based on 1 Corinthians 7:1-5. Our prayer is that these will be just the beginning of a on-going conversation about sex with your spouse. The more you talk about sex, the easier it will be to talk about sex.

Ask each other:

1. Before we were married, what role did you think sex would play in our marriage?
2. Now that we're married, has your view changed?
3. Is sexual temptation something you experience? How often? What form does it usually take? How can I help?
4. What pops out at you from 1 Corinthians 7:1-5? Why?
5. What does our sex life look like for you in the future? In the next year? In the next 5 years?

We encourage you to push past your fears and talk about, well, you know what, with your spouse, the one you married and promised to love and cherish.

Bible Thought: God is not afraid to talk about sex. In

fact, he dedicates an entire book to it to highlight the importance of sex in marriage.

PRAYER: Father, help me not to be embarrassed to talk about sex with my spouse. Help us to be open and free to talk about this important subject. In Jesus' name. Amen.

DAY 36 - THE MARITAL RIGHTS OF THE WIFE

The husband should give to his wife her conjugal rights, and likewise the wife to her husband. (1 Corinthians 7:3 ESV)

Conjugal rights, or sexual rights, are a protection for the benefit of the wife as well as the husband. Paul encourages husbands to make sure they fulfill their conjugal responsibilities to their wives first and then, secondly, encourages wives similarly.

Every word, and the placement of every word, in the Bible is strategic. Young's Literal Translation puts it like this, *"To the wife* let the husband the due benevolence render," (emphasis added). The sentence starts **"To the wife"** suggesting that husbands were neglecting their wives in this area in Corinth.

This verse makes it clear that the conjugal rights of a

wife are not to be neglected by her husband. She is to receive the attention she deserves from her husband.

Not Just for the Husband

Yes, the husband usually has the stronger sex drive, although not always, but his sexual aggression should not be mistaken for needing sex more than his wife.

The sex drive per se has nothing to do with sexual need and fulfillment. Sex fulfills many things and we make a mistake of thinking that it's for physical release only. When we think this way then we wrongly conclude that sex is primarily for the man.

But sex is more than a physical release. It involves the body, yes, but also the soul and spirit. Sex is a renewal of a spiritual covenant, brings order to the chaos of the day, reconnects the disconnected husband and wife, fulfills an intense emotional need in both, and re-establishes an exclusive relationship.

The problem is when wives don't generally think of sex as a need or at least as a need like their husband. God's Word suggests sexual intimacy is a need of the wife as well as the husband, just different.

God's Moral Law and Conjugal Rights

Let's look at a curious passage in Exodus. This is God's moral law concerning the conjugal rights of the wife. It is not binding now of course but clearly expresses what God considers right and just about a wife's conjugal rights.

> *If he marries another woman, she retains all her full rights to meals, clothing, and marital relations. If he won't do any of these three things for her, she goes free, for nothing. (Exodus 21:7-11 MSG)*

In summary, if a man bought a Hebrew woman as a slave to be his wife and then decided to marry again, he could not diminish her conjugal rights but would have to maintain the same frequency of sex as before he took a second wife.

For example, if the first wife was used to sex twice a week, he was obligated to continue the same frequency. If he didn't maintain the same frequency, she could go to the authorities with her complaint.

This is the Old Covenant, of course, but it points out God's concern for the wife's conjugal rights.

BIBLE THOUGHT: God is very concerned about the conjugal rights of wives.

PRAYER: Father, help me to see sex from a biblical perspective instead of from the perspective of today's culture. In Jesus' name. Amen.

DAY 37 - THE FIRST COMMAND OF GOD TO HIS CHILDREN

And God said to them, "Be fruitful and multiply and fill the earth" (Genesis 1:28a ESV)

The "Law of First Mention" is a hermeneutics term that refers to the importance of the first instance of a word, topic, idea, or doctrine in the Bible. The Law says that, more often than not, the first mention sets the foundation for the interpretation of all other mentions. It therefore tends to carry more weight in the interpretation of any passage about a particular word, topic, idea, or doctrine.

Genesis is a "book of beginnings" and introduces many topics and doctrines of the Bible. It holds a special place in the hermeneutical world of interpretation. Let's look at a couple significant "first mentions" in Genesis.

. . .

The First Institution **Defined by God**: Marriage

God didn't waste any time to give us his first institution. He describes marriage as, "a man shall leave his father and his mother and hold fast to his wife, and they shall become one flesh". God's definition of marriage emphasizes the physical nature of marriage - "one flesh". (Genesis 2:24)

God created the world and everything in it and immediately instituted marriage and told Adam and Eve to "be fruitful and multiply". It seems even to the casual observer that God thinks marriage and married sex is important to his plan for mankind, before and after the Fall. Groucho Marx famously said, "Marriage is a wonderful institution, but who wants to live in an institution?" Well, God thinks it's good place for his children to find comfort, companionship, and fulfillment.

The First Command **of God to His Children**: Have lots of sex and produce lots of children.

It's interesting that God's very first command to his children was to play in the Garden of Eden! In effect he says to get frisky, enjoy one another, and "fill the earth" with your offspring. He *then* says subdue the earth.

First Explanation **of the Structure of Marriage from God**

God defines marriage as "one flesh" and he gives us the structure of marriage as complementarian when he says, "Then the Lord God said, "It is not good that the man should be alone; I will make him a helper fit for him." (Genesis 2:18)

Nobody wants to be the "helper" because it sounds like you do all the work and get none of the credit! We get it but God's way is the best way even when it doesn't seem "fair" by our standards. His ways are higher than our ways and that's a very good thing.

For all you egalitarians out there, God's Word says that the bedroom is the most egalitarian place on the planet! (This is explained in our book, "Radical Sex: God's Foundation for a Healthy Marriage".)

In summary, God's first institution highlights physical intimacy and his first command calls for lots of physical intimacy. This speaks volumes to the place of sex in marriage. When we try to push sex to the periphery of marriage, the Word always brings us back to God's original message that sex is central, not peripheral, to a biblical marriage.

BIBLE THOUGHT: The first institution God created was marriage. God's first command to those in "The Institution" was to have lots of sex.

PRAYER: Father, help me to understand why you think the centrality of sex in marriage is so important. In Jesus' name. Amen.

DAY 38 - JOYFULLY STUCK!

Therefore a man shall leave his father and his mother and hold fast to his wife, and they shall become one flesh. (Genesis 2:24 ESV)

Krazy Glue is ethyl cyanoacrylate - "a non-toxic, colorless, extremely fast-acting, strong adhesive. It can lift "2000 pounds per square inch" according to the company website. It is one of the fastest acting and strongest glues available. But it takes a "trigger" to activate its stickiness; that trigger is water "which is found on nearly every surface in the world".

Marriage is the strongest and closest of all human relationships. And, like Krazy Glue, it requires a catalyst to activate the adhesive properties. The catalyst for marriage is sex - the first time to consummate the marriage and each subsequent time to reinforce the bond.

The Hebrew word for "hold fast" is "cleave" in the King James Version. It's a term used elsewhere in the Bible to describe the sticky quality of a covenant relationship. It means "being intertwined" or "stuck together". It has the idea of two pieces of paper being glued together. If you try to separate the papers after the glue has dried, you just end up with a shredded mess.

God defines marriage as "stuck" together as in "one flesh". These are the two principle elements of marriage after "leaving" parents.

> "Hold fast *to his wife, and they shall become* one flesh." *(Emphasis added)*

In other words, once married you are stuck to each other. This is more than a physical oneness, there is a spiritual oneness also, although God highlights the physical connection to illustrate the spiritual connection. (See 1 Corinthians 6:16-20)

STUCK for Life

Once we realize the "stuckness" of our relationship, we understand that this is for life as in "for better or worse, 'til death do us part". We now have a choice to stay stuck joyfully or to stay stuck miserably or something in-between. The choice is ours as a couple, although we realize it takes two in agreement to make a "cleaving marriage" as opposed to a "leaving marriage".

God, through his definition of marriage, is telling us that the satisfaction in marriage is not necessarily tied to what we would normally think. We think a satisfying marriage requires _____ (fill in the blank). God says a satisfying marriage is leaving, cleaving, and becoming "one flesh".

The question then becomes: How can we stay stuck together joyfully? Well, here's three ideas around God's definition of marriage - leave, cleave, and one flesh.

1. Consider your relationship with your spouse as your number one priority in life because the relationship between a husband and a wife is the closest human relationship on earth. Do not put any relationship above your spouse, except Christ, including your parents, children, or other family members.
2. "Hold fast" to your spouse with all your might because you are stuck with each other for life. This is good thing. It's an intentional God thing. He meant it for your joy and his glory so hang on and enjoy life together. In other words, don't give up easily.
3. Consider physical intimacy as God's primary means to keep the relationship stuck together for life.

Marriage either thrives or dies. God wants us to thrive in marriage, and in life, by agreeing with his Word and trusting him to help us through the rough times.

. . .

BIBLE THOUGHT: God wants us to be joyfully stuck to our spouse.

PRAYER: Father, help me to define marriage as you define marriage. In Jesus' name. Amen.

DAY 39 - NOT IN THE MOOD

Do not deprive one another *(1 Corinthians 7:5a ESV)*

There are probably many valid reasons for telling your spouse "Not now, dear" from illness to PTO meetings and everything in-between. However, all things being equal, "Not now, honey" usually means "I'm not in the mood". Paul tells us, as we have seen numerous times in our journey toward a more biblical married sex life, that we have conjugal responsibilities toward our spouse. Paul's imperative, "Do not deprive!", is there because Paul knows we tend to deprive.

THE RESPONSE

"Not in the mood" is not a biblical response. If we

wait for both of us to be "in the mood", at the same time, then it could be long wait. We're usually not in the mood because we are looking at ourselves and not our spouse.

The only biblical response to a request is an enthusiastic, "Yes!" This seems unreasonable in so many ways especially in our culture of individualism. How can anyone, realistically, be in the mood all the time? If you go by your feelings then it's impossible.

God's Word tells us clearly that we should be *ready* for sex. This goes beyond feelings to obedience. The Word says be ready for your spouse when *they're* in the mood. You have conjugal responsibilities, do not deprive.

How can you be ready?

1. Don't be surprised when your spouse suggests sex! Many are startled when their spouse says the secret word and panic, "Now!?" Be ready, don't be surprised.
2. Anticipate when your spouse will be in the mood. If you've been married for any length of time then you should know your spouse's sexual rhythms. Anticipate.
3. Make sex a priority - think about it, talk about it, plan it. Yes, there are many obstacles to the one flesh reality of marriage including illness, aging, and travel and so many more. But make the effort to make sex a priority.
4. Change your mind about sex and align it with God's Word and not the culture. We like the way JB Phillips puts it, "Don't let the world

around you squeeze you into its own mold."
(Romans 12:2)

When we put God's way into practice then we will know God's plan is good but not before.

Bible Thought: God's way has to be practiced in order to discover that it is the best way.

Prayer: Father, help my mind to be transformed from cultural biases to God's truth about married sex. In Jesus' name. Amen.

DAY 40 - GOD SEES US AS ONE

So ought men to love their wives as their own bodies. He that loveth his wife loveth himself. For no man ever yet hated his own flesh; but nourisheth and cherisheth it, even as the Lord the church: For we are members of his body, of his flesh, and of his bones. For this cause shall a man leave his father and mother, and shall be joined unto his wife, and they two shall be one flesh. (Ephesians 5:28-31 KJV)

Type "Health Benefits of Sex" into Google and you get 618 million results. It's well documented that there are many health benefits of sex and more are discovered seemingly every day. It's exactly like

God to design something that feels good and is good for you!

Here's one of many health benefits God built into sex according to a recent WebMD article:

"Bonds You to Your Partner - The hormone oxytocin is released during sex, and it sparks feelings of intimacy, affection, and closeness with your partner. That helps build a strong, stable relationship, which is good for everyone."

Bonded

God goes beyond *bonding* to *bonded*. When you're married, God no longer sees you as two individuals only but now you are bonded as "one flesh". It's not like you morphed into a hybrid being like in a sci-fi movie but your status has changed from "individual" to "couple".

As a married couple, if you hate your wife, you are actually hating yourself. Paul tells husbands to love your wife because your wife is your "own flesh". He illustrates the point by revealing we are members of Christ's body - "of his flesh, and of his bones". There is a spiritual as well as physical aspect of our marriage relationship. In fact, Pauls reveals that marital intimacy reflects Christ and his church.

God Sees Us as One

We are rugged individuals, captains of our own ship, and makers of our own destiny. Marriage, our culture tells us, is two individuals coming together for the purpose of supporting each other's aspirations. We help one another along life's journey but remain two individuals. Sex is healthy but nothing beyond a physical release, the world says.

God sees us as one. When one is blessed, then both are blessed. When one is gifted, then both are gifted. When one is hurting then both are hurting. When you yell at your wife, you are yelling at yourself. Paul tells us not to hate our wives because it's the same as hating ourselves and no one hates themselves.

What we do to the other, we do to ourselves. If we hurt the other, we hurt ourselves. If we love the other, we love ourselves. If we deny sex to the other then we deny sex to ourselves and all its benefits.

Beyond Health Benefits of Sex

Bonding, as we have seen, is one of the many health benefits of sex. Other health benefits of sex include sharper minds, stronger immune system, more energy, pain relief, loss of weight, lower stress, longer life, and better sleep.

When we deny intimacy to our spouse, then we are not only denying the many health benefits of sex but we are eroding the bond that God wants sex to create in his "one flesh" masterpiece called marriage.

Bible Thought: There are many benefits to sex and we hurt ourselves if we deny to our spouse.

. . .

Prayer: Father, help me to properly understand the benefits of sex for my marriage. In Jesus' name. Amen.

AFTERWORD

AN INVITATION TO FOLLOW JESUS

We have tried to show you how God sees marriage and how he wants every marriage to grow in grace and intimacy. And those of you who know Jesus personally, you may have discovered your heart beating a little faster as you read about God's mystery of a man and a woman in marriage.

May God grant that those of you who have never said "Yes" to the Spirit's call to follow Jesus, may now say, "Yes, I believe his Word, I will listen to the Holy Spirit, and turn and follow Jesus Christ, the One who died for me and took all my sins on himself. He has won my heart by his great love for me and the revelation of his kindness through his blessed Word."

If you have a testimony to share after reading this book, please send it to us via email THEBIBLESEXDEVOTIONAL@GMAIL.COM.

Thank you and may God bless your marriage richly.

NOTES

INTRODUCTION

1. Keller, "The Meaning of Marriage", page 267

DAY 7 - SEX & SANCTIFICATION

1. https://thebiblesexdevotional.com/

DAY 13 - CASUAL SEX

1. https://nypost.com/2018/05/06/netflix-is-killing-couples-sex-lives-study/

DAY 17 - THE DEATH OF SEX

1. https://www.deseretnews.com/article/865629093/US-marriage-rate-hits-new-low-and-may-continue-to-decline.html
2. https://www.washingtonpost.com/news/to-your-health/wp/2017/06/30/the-u-s-fertility-rate-just-hit-a-historic-low-why-some-demographers-are-freaking-out/?noredirect=on&utm_term=.f0a26bdab1ff
3. https://www.sciencedaily.com/releases/2017/03/170307112903.htm
4. http://tyglobalist.org/in-the-magazine/features/single-and-sexless-celibacy-syndrome-in-japan/

ABOUT THE AUTHORS

René and Gloria Vallières have been followers of Jesus for 40 years and married for 48 years with three grown children and six grandchildren. René was a pastor with the Christian and Missionary Alliance and later a teaching elder in New York and Utah evangelical fellowships. Gloria has a prayer ministry and has published articles in both secular and Christian journals.

René and Gloria propose that the answer to the confusion in marriage is a radically biblical approach to sexual intimacy. The couple has decades in Christian ministry and experience teaching about relationships. They seek to remove the cloud over married sex with their books, *Radical Sex: God's Foundation for a Healthy Marriage*; *The 40 Day Bible Sex Devotional for Christian Couples*, and *The 14 Day Bible Sex Devotional for Christian Couples* (eBook only).

facebook.com/thebiblesexdevotional
twitter.com/thebiblesexdev
instagram.com/thebiblesexdevotional

Made in the USA
Columbia, SC
07 October 2020